C.O.C

CHRISTIAN

RESCO

Tel: 07932 159750

This item is the property of C.O.C. and is loaned for a
period of two weeks. It is a requirement that any person
to whom this item is loaned MUST return it to C.O.C.
on or before the latest date shown below.

A Christian Woman book
Birthright?

Maureen Long is a
freelance writer and journalist,
who is deeply concerned with social issues.
She lives in Lowestoft, Suffolk,
and has three children and
several grandchildren.

Christian Woman books

Other titles in preparation

Birthright?

A Christian woman looks at abortion

MAUREEN LONG

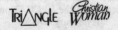

First published 1985
Triangle
SPCK
Holy Trinity Church
Marylebone Road
London NW1 4DU

British Library Cataloguing in Publication Data

Long, Maureen
    Birthright? : a Christian woman looks at
    abortion. – (Christian woman series)
    1. Abortion – Religious aspects – Christianity
    I. Title II. Series
    261.8'3   HQ767.3

    ISBN 0–281–04196–2

Typeset by Inforum Ltd
Printed in Great Britain by
Hazell, Watson & Viney Limited
Member of the BPCC Group
Aylesbury, Bucks

To all women

and especially to the memory of my own mother
who gave to five of us birth,
love and happiness

Contents

Contents

Editor's Foreword

Christian women are developing a new awareness of the way our faith touches every part of our lives. Women who have always lived in a Christian environment are facing up to the important issues in the world around them. Women who have found in Christ a new direction for living are seeking to sort out the problems that are hampering their spiritual growth. And many women are rediscovering the joy in using their God-given talents, in their relationships with God and with other people, and in their spiritual lives and worship. *Christian Woman* magazine has been privileged to be part of this learning process.

As a result of this deepening awareness and commitment to Christianity, many books have been published which help women to sort out what God can do for them as women, as wives, as career people, as mothers, as single women. Most of these books however have been rooted in the American culture; this *Christian Woman* series has come into being because we believe it is important that we have books that talk our own language, and are relevant to everyday life in our own culture.

Each book in this series will deal with some aspect of living as a Christian woman in today's world. I am delighted that we have been able to be part of the blossoming of God's church in this way. We hope that the books will help you as a Christian woman to overcome problems, enrich your life and your relationships, learn more of God, think through important issues, enjoy your femininity, make wise choices, and deepen your commitment to Jesus Christ.

In these books we have invited people to share what they have learned about living as Christians. Not everyone will agree with all the ideas expressed in each book, but I know that you will find every book in the series interesting and thought-provoking.

Books change people's lives – perhaps these books will change your life.

GAIL LAWTHER

x

Acknowledgements

A big thank you to Alison Davis and her filing system, and particularly for her contribution to chapter 9 of this book.

My special thanks also to other contributors:
Nancy Hopkins for her poem, *The Innocents – Unborn*;
Noreen Riols for her moving contribution to chapter 4;
and all others, named and unnamed, who have helped with this book by generously sharing their professional expertise and personal experiences.

Biblical quotations throughout are taken from the Holy Bible, New International Version, copyright © 1973, 1978, 1984, International Bible Society, and are used by permission.

Frequent reference has been made to *The Tiniest Humans* by Professor Jerome Lejeune and Professor Sir Albert William Liley, edited and published by Robert L. Sassone of Santa Ana, California, USA, copyright © Robert L. Sassone 1977.

The Innocents – Unborn

We are the voiceless ones
borrowing your tongues.
We are the sightless ones
blinded by men without vision.
We are the unwanted ones,
precipitated into momentary light;
deposited in fire-lined cradles;
smothered, our infantile gasp;
coffined our imprisoned cry,
a whimper that escaping
rises to a ghostly wail
haunting our cities.
The Holy Innocents were mourned;
our massacre is condoned.
Herod's hands are clinically clean.
We are the condemned ones;
society our executioners.
We are the voiceless ones;
lend us your tongues.

NANCY HOPKINS

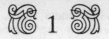

1

'Why Me?'

Bells rang and sirens hooted across the frosty night, their echoes dimly heard through the solid walls of the large church. Through the concentration of prayer, they marked the mysterious division of the Old Year and the New. Thoughts alternated, as had the minister's prayers, between thanksgiving for all that was past, and trust for the unknown days to come. Each close member of the family and those with special needs were brought to God and especially remembered.

The watchnight service ended. My daughter turned beside me, whispering 'Happy New Year'. That 'peace that passes understanding' rose up joyously as I returned her greeting. I was thankful, for the first time for several years, to be with her, her husband and two small sons for the end of the Christmas celebrations. She is our only daughter, doubly precious because her coming had been a complete surprise. As she turned back to greet friends of her church 'family' the thought came to me that the Orwellian year of 1984 had passed into history. I found myself drawn into a warm circle of Christians of like mind, introduced to new faces, all the while knowing that these people had 'old' values. The church door opened, the clear air rushed in, bells clanged noisily, hurrying footsteps and friendly greetings, love and laughter surrounded us as we walked briskly back. So much for Orwell!   And yet . . .

Later, lying in the darkness of the unfamiliar room, major events of the year rushed to mind: a car accident in

1

the family, parties, the miners' strike, grandchildren going to new schools, a new baby; the Warnock Report on human fertilisation and embryology; Victoria Gillick's success in presenting a petition to Parliament containing more signatures than at any time since the abolition of slavery, then her second success in the High Court, to ensure that no girl under sixteen years old is given the contraceptive pill without her parents' knowledge; the resultant hue and cry from the media and the medical profession. At the end of another celebration of the birth of the Christ-child, at the start of International Year of Youth, the newspapers were decrying Mrs Gillick's success: 'More unwanted pregnancies!' 'What of the girl with uncaring parents?' 'Return of the back-street abortionists!'

The tight knot of anger churned again in my stomach as I prayed and tried to recapture that earlier peace. What kind of 'Big Brother' lurked at the opening of 1985? What subtle hazards surrounded the path into the unknown? I snuggled lower into the warmth of the comfortable bed, thanked God again for my daughter . . . and was again back in memory between the high white walls of the hospital ward, tasting the lingering effects of ether, remembering the shock at hearing that I had given birth to twins, the two together weighing less than the average 'normal' baby I had thought I was carrying. Back in that premature unit of over thirty years ago, seeing my babies for the first time through glass (*in vitro*?) watching them being fed through a tube into their stomachs, reliving the thoughts and feelings of young motherhood, I agonised over today's babies.

I had been brought up to revere all life. Live birds had to be rescued from the family cat! Even as a child, I knew that only God could give life or should take it.

When my adored Gran died, I was an evacuee, in my first year at grammar school. I accepted her death naturally. She had been ill, and old people do die. It was a fact of life. I had been prepared for it gently, by my parents' letters and

2

by my 'billet mother', who was in their confidence.

My mother's premature death from an incurable disease, when I was eighteen, was a different matter. She was forty-two. The local doctor had diagnosed food poisoning. It was only because we were moving house that she had to be taken to our former home town, where our old doctor recognised the symptoms and rushed her into hospital. It was too late. She died two days later. In those seventy-two hours from diagnosis until death, the truth hit me like a cannon ball: we are powerless against the strength or the weakness of that mysterious thread we call life.

I had a strong faith, an inner source of power in prayer and Bible study, the back-up of a marvellous church and Christian friends. I knew that God was in charge, and in my young idealism never once questioned his will. There had been prayer over those three days from many churches and people, friends and strangers, Christians and non-Christians, but God had chosen not to allow her to live.

I had not missed her as much as I thought I would, during my pregnancy. She had done her work well. The eldest of five children, I had always known a baby in the house or family circle. I instinctively knew what to prepare and do, but I was not prepared for being whisked off to hospital at the end of the seventh month to give birth prematurely. (It is agonising for me to realise that at that gestational age, babies today have been destroyed.)

I needed my mother then. Thoughts of her death accentuated my fears for that slender thread of life to which our babies were clinging. God couldn't take them from us, could he? Our son was the smaller, but the stronger. One caring sister called him her 'teeniest, weeniest', and gave him special cuddles after I left hospital. Our daughter, eight ounces heavier, was nevertheless the one who caused concern. We were warned that she might not survive, that the first three weeks were the most critical. Those twenty-one days were like an eternity of constant prayer, living for

3

the minute, afraid to plan, yet needing to double up on the existing layette. I knitted and sewed, warned the shop that our order might be changed to a twin pram and extra cot and high chair and promised God incessantly that if our babies were spared to us they would be given a Christian home and every opportunity to find him as the loving Father, personal Saviour and motivating Spirit who had kept us going throughout that period.

The premature ward was a bit different from those of 1984. Eight sets of twins and a few other babies took up the modern incubators. I was an emergency, not booked into the already overflowing maternity unit. Our babies were in an older, 'spare' incubator called 'the cucumber frame' by the staff, who joked about my husband being a market gardener and able to rear baby things in frames. From the beginning they were dressed warmly in coats and leggings, bonnets, bootees and mitts. Only their tiny faces were visible and they were beautiful. It was easier to hope then, until the first time I saw them undressed. Their 'old men' wizened heads and pot tummies, thin arms and legs sent me back down to the depths of despair and to renewed pleading and bargaining with God.

I felt helpless. I was prepared to give and do the utmost for my babies, but I could not give them *life*. That was a unique and precious gift, given or taken only by God. The sacredness of life was deeply and irrevocably accepted as I went through both my mother's death and those first weeks of my baby twins' life. To this day, I consider my children a precious gift from God, my own life an opportunity to be committed to him. It is human to fail, to let the pressures, the worldliness, the expediency of society infiltrate our highest ideals, but at the core of the Christian's commitment is the root idea that we are God's and he is ours. Our life, our destiny, our times and seasons are in his hands. He is the Giver and Sustainer of life, that mystical, unimaginable secret thread that physically motivates each person from conception to death.

Two years later our twins were joined by a baby brother. This birth was short, sharp, natural and took place at home. Two hours after the first labour pains woke me, our son was in my arms. I was bursting with happiness that he was full-term, beautiful and full of life. This time there was no agonising wait for each quarter-ounce of gained weight to be treasured in hope, no expressing and boiling milk, sterilising bottles and dispatching it on the bus to the city hospital daily, and later, no test-weighing before and after each breast-feed, no bargaining with God, but a deep commitment to his will for our lives and those of our children.

A few years later, for the first time, I witnessed the birth of someone else's baby. It was a moving and humbling experience. Although the midwife had delivered hundreds of babies, she admitted to the same feeling of human dependence on God, of helplessness, then sudden elation when everything was all right and the baby born safely with no complications. That night she told me that most women, at the moment of their babies' birth say, 'Thank God' reverently and with deep feeling.

As the tiny face of my newest nephew wrinkled into his first cry, I too was thanking God.

From this 'gut feeling' of awe and wonder at the miracle of new life, of a deep trust in God as the perpetual sustainer of our existence, arose the first knot of anger and fear as the proposals for the 1967 Abortion Act were put forward. It seemed impossible that the Parliament of our great Christian country could allow such a bill to become law. Looking back, we can see with sorrow how many sections of the Church failed to fight the proposals. Some mainstream churches were too busy with unity proposals; some did scratch at the surface of the problem; but no real concentrated Christian effort was made to abort the bill. At that time, to many in the Church, even the mention of abortion

5

was 'not very nice'. 'There's nothing we can do about it' was the average feeling. The Church in general was too respectable, or too apathetic, to dabble in such subjects and is now seeing the results. As Edmund Burke pointed out, all that is necessary for the triumph of evil is for good men to do nothing.

That is, literally, what the majority of British Christians did about the 1967 Abortion Act, myself, to my shame, among them. Because of the 'social clause' in the Act, we were suddenly a nation witnessing abortion on demand.

That period was called 'the swinging sixties'. It was the heyday of the flower power people, of mass rallies of teenagers, of the advent of the contraceptive pill, of women's liberation, of drug trafficking, of the 'new morality' where guilt was a dirty word and sin had been abolished from the vocabulary. Many of these so-called freedoms promoted the climate in which the Act was passed. The teenagers of that time are the parents of today's teenagers, many of whom are now seeking abortions, often with parental knowledge and consent, sometimes even with pressure from their parents who feel unable to cope with an unmarried daughter and a first grandchild.

What has happened to the concept that all life is sacred?

When did we stop calling an unborn child a baby and start calling it a foetus?

The subtle change in attitude is one dangerous offshoot of the Act. It was Dean Inge who said, 'The Church that is married to the spirit of the age faces widowhood in the next.'

Only slowly are the Church and Christians in general awakening to the fact that a gradual but inevitable change is taking place in the thinking and attitudes of many in this country today.

The pro-Life groups drew up a petition to Parliament objecting to some of the proposals of the Warnock Commission which reported on the latest developments and proposals concerning human fertilisation and embryology and opened the way to experiments on human embryos. Copies of the petition on our shop counter produced numerous reactions. I was staggered by some of the remarks. I had expected that those of my own generation would mostly sign it and I was not disappointed. The usual comment here was, 'God knows best. We shouldn't mess around with nature.'

Also expected was the indifference of many of the older age-group. Obviously there were exceptions but the general feeling was: 'Those things shouldn't be talked about. That's where all the trouble has started.' 'They won't listen to us, anyway.'

'It won't affect me. I won't be here to know what happens.' 'They'll blow the world to bits first anyway, so what does it matter?'

I suppose I had also expected that the more avant garde mothers of today's teenagers would be in favour of any experimentation, regardless of the consequences for the child, since they were products of those swinging sixties, and pre-conditioned to believe that: 'It's not really a baby at that stage.' 'Experiments can help others.' 'There are already too many mouths to feed in the world.'

The big surprise was the reaction of some of today's young people to the proposals. Many wanted to sign. Some were sorry that being under sixteen, they were not old enough to do so. What is the cause of their attitude? Most of their parents were against signing. Is it the all-round education they receive, school sex lessons where they are taught that life begins at conception, or the hard work done in schools and youth clubs by speakers from pro-Life groups? I am not able to draw any fair conclusion, but it was an encouraging sign. (Maybe the ones who thought otherwise kept silent.) I believe there is hope for the future, but that does not mean we can sit back and do nothing. Janet, who works for the organisation LIFE, told me that she is

7

only able to speak to sixth form pupils in schools; but girls are having abortions well before the sixth form, and there is a need to start teaching the sanctity and wonder of life in the womb much earlier in schools and youth clubs.

At this time, the whole subject of how far we should go as regards tampering with, experimenting on or controlling the life of the unborn, is of vital importance. Foetology and genetics are unfolding wonders and possibilities that stagger scientists and maybe make them too adventurous. It is imperative that the Church should spell out clearly where it stands. The Church, though, is you and me. Science and medical practice are racing ahead of our thinking and of social ethics. There is a strong lobby of pro-abortionists in this country. The British Medical Association is finding its membership split down the middle in the aftermath of Victoria Gillick's High Court victory. Many conscientious family doctors are worried. It is time for the whole Church, not just its leaders, to take a good look at the entire spectrum of the abortion question and how it affects each section of the community: families, doctors, gynaecologists, parents, medical researchers, churches, the handicapped and our individual Christian conscience.

In this book, I am attempting to look at some of the issues as they affect the average family today. If you believe that God created the world and made each human being completely individual, that each of us has an immortal part that lives on after death, that God cares about what we do with his creation, then please stay with me. If you believe part or even none of these, then please read on. Every day we are learning and absorbing new experiences, new ideas. Our century has seen the most rapid rate of change since the world began: from the first flying machine to a man on the moon, from foot soldiers to guided missiles. We have to constantly think and rethink our position on moral issues. With regard to abortion, I know where I stand. I do not know if you, the reader, are alongside me, or whether we are a little distant or poles apart, but we can have a dialogue, not because I am an expert on the subject, but because increasingly over past years God has been nudging me to do something about it. At times lately, that 'nudge' has seemed more like a headlong plunge into the subject, but I have surfaced, still believing in the sanctity of life and the strength of love. Please plunge in, too.

Mother Teresa has said, 'To me, the nations with legalised abortions are the poorer nations. The great destroyer of peace today is the crime against the innocent unborn child.'

That statement takes some thinking through. Maybe we had thought it was sophisticated weaponry, or lack of trust between the leaders of the great powers, or even commercial vested interest in the arms trade, that was destroying our peace; but taken all the way back, we are thinking about human beings.

What is so special about *them*?

St John begins his brilliant description of the coming of the Lord Jesus Christ into the world thus:

> In the beginning was the Word, and the Word was with God, and the Word was God. He was with God in the beginning. Through him all things were made; without him nothing was made that has been made. In him was *life*, and that life was the light of men. The light shines in the darkness, but the darkness has not understood it . . . The true light that gives light to every man was coming into the world (John 1.1–5, 9, italics mine).

So God created everything and everybody.

He 'lights' or shows and lights up the way of everybody.

But that is not all. When, as Charles Wesley so succinctly put it, 'Our God, contracted to a span,' was 'incomprehensibly made man', he came to earth as a holy conceptus, whom his mother, Mary, carried full-term.

He entered human life from the beginning. He experienced life in the womb, with all its wonderful developments, some of which scientists are only just beginning to show us. The Bible declares indisputably that his life on earth began at conception.

The Apostles' Creed declares that he was 'conceived by the Holy Ghost, born of the virgin Mary'.

Life in the womb is so precious, so human, so integral a part of our existence, that God himself was unable to become truly man without experiencing it. The infinite, all-creating God could have introduced his Son at any human stage, as a child, an adult, or as an angel-type, but he sent him as a conceptus, at the very start of his human life.

How, then, can we as Christians stand on the sidelines as powerful pro-abortion forces water down or completely disregard a divine creativity (and an ultimate judgement!), as millions of lives are wantonly destroyed by abortion and scientific experimentation each year in our world, to which Christ came to enlighten us?

That is what is so special about us. God not only created us, but he sent Jesus to show us the way, and his Spirit to enable us to live in that way.

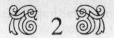

2

Abortion:
How and When is it Performed?

In the United Kingdom each year there are over 150,000 legal abortions. How and why are they performed and what gestational age are the babies?

The 'social reasons' clause in the 1967 Abortion Act gives carte blanche to most women requesting a termination of a pregnancy. 'Risk to the mother's physical or mental health' seems to include natural anxiety at the thought of pregnancy on the part of an unmarried mother, a wife pregnant as the result of an extra-marital affair or a mother worried about the financial problems of having another child. An abortion may also be performed if a new baby would affect the physical or mental health of other children in that family. As can easily be seen, these reasons can have an elastic interpretation.

Many parents or grandparents will have known of a pregnancy in the family circle which has initially aroused panic and problems. Countless mothers have felt dismay at the prospect of another mouth to feed, especially in the days before birth control was widely used, and before the Welfare State took over the responsibility of doctors' and nurses' fees and unemployment or sick benefit. However, by the time most of these babies have been born, there has been acceptance and joy at the birth. Nature gives a woman time to think and plan. The decision to abort, on the other hand, is usually made in a short space of time while the

11

initial panic is still on. Some impetuous decisions are made and subsequently regretted.

Blame has to be apportioned to the current social climate and also to the carefully chosen language of the pro-abortion lobby. In my grandmother's time a pregnant woman was described as being 'with child': a truly biblical description! My mother and her contemporaries were 'in the family way'. I was 'going to have a baby' or 'expecting'. My children and their peers were 'pregnant'.

As the language changes there is often a slight shift in emphasis. Lately, people have tended to leave the child out of the description, so that expecting a baby becomes purely an impersonal medical state. The baby has become the 'foetus'; and an abortion, that word formerly associated with backstreet operators and shame, is a 'termination of pregnancy'. The most insidious and dangerous change of all is in the carefully programmed shift from reverence for the sanctity of life to assessment of the 'quality of life', but more of that later.

The majority of abortions (about 110,000 annually) are performed before the mother is twelve weeks pregnant. This alone indicates the time pressure on the mother. In a matter of a week or two after the confirmation of the new life within her, it has often been annihilated. The decision has to be taken when she is usually not feeling very well. It is the period for morning sickness (for most women the first three months are the worst, physically). She is naturally worried and she may well be under pressure from her parents, her boyfriend if she is unmarried, or perhaps her husband, pushing her to make an instant decision.

If she decides on abortion, how is it carried out?

There are five methods currently used, and a new one just becoming known.

1   *Dilatation and curettage* (D and C) involves the use of the curette, a sharp instrument like a tiny hoe, which is inserted through the stretched cervix (the neck of the

12

uterus). The wall of the uterus is then scraped, destroying the baby in the process. This method has mostly been superseded by:

2 *The suction method* was first used in China where abortion was legal long before it was here. A powerful suction pipe is inserted into the uterus through the cervix, and the embryo and placenta are sucked out.

These first two methods are used in the first twelve weeks, but approximately 20,000 abortions are performed in Britain each year later than twelve weeks of pregnancy. There are three methods used to destroy these larger babies.

3 *Salt poisoning* abortion occurs when a strong salt solution is injected through the mother's abdomen into the 'bag of water' or sac containing the baby surrounded by his/her amniotic fluid. The child swallows the salt and is poisoned. His skin is burned. The mother goes into labour the next day, delivering a shrivelled, hideously-scarred dead baby.

Approximately 1,500–2,000 terminations are 'late abortions' done after the twentieth week of pregnancy. Two further methods are used at this stage.

4 *Hysterotomy* (not to be confused with hysterectomy, removal of the womb), is abortion by caesarean section. The baby is removed surgically, is almost always alive and is subsequently 'allowed to die' or deliberately helped to die.

It seems inconceivable that a surgeon and nursing staff can stand aside and allow a baby to die in these circumstances, because it is 'unwanted' by the mother for social, psychological or financial reasons, while the 'wanted' prematurely-born or surgically removed baby is rushed into the intensive care unit. At this point of differentiation, the doctor becomes, not an instrument of healing, but a tool of society. Here, the sanctity of life is superseded by the 'quality of life' concept. Yet the doctor has no means of assessing the future of either of these babies. We cannot forecast a child's future quality of life as we try to forecast tomorrow's weather! The current criteria are social, not moral, ethics.

5   The other method for larger babies has been *prostaglandin abortion*, where a powerful drug is injected or applied to the womb muscle, causing it to contract violently, expelling the child. There are side effects: cardiac arrest, low blood pressure, nausea, vomiting, diarrhoea, flushing, shivering, headache, dizziness, temporary fever, raised white cell count, for the mother; sometimes dismemberment of the baby.

It should be noted that a human foetus is extremely strong, as has been seen in the way babies have survived severe accidents before birth, and any method of abortion has to be powerful to dislodge the baby from the womb, let alone expel it from the mother, hence such strong methods, especially for larger, healthy babies.

Progesterone is a key hormone in the miracle of human pregnancy. Work is now going on to produce anti-progesterone drugs, which could bring on menstruation, interrupt pregnancy and 'may lead to a revision of our concepts of abortion' (David L. Healy, *British Medical Journal* 23 February 1985).

In November 1984 the CIBA Foundation held a symposium on the medical progress of and social implications of abortion. Amongst other topics, preliminary experiments with prostaglandins E and F used with anti-progesterone drugs were discussed. It was said that RU 486, an anti-progesterone (see below, method 6), could also be used with prostaglandin so that smaller doses of each could be given, minimising the side effects of larger doses needed to dislodge a larger baby. The first could be used to separate the child from the mother, the second to 'evacuate the womb'.

Several pharmaceutical companies have given priority to developing these new drugs. E.E. Baulieu's paper to the CIBA gathering said that if these are proved competent they 'will herald a new contra-gestational approach to fertility control and raise several critical medical, moral and legal questions.' (*BMJ* 23 February 1985.)

6   A new French pill developed by Roussell-Eclat using RU 486 could open up the horrific possibilities of 'do it yourself' abortion. It will terminate a pregnancy by medical rather than surgical means, at a very early date, probably before the eighth week. The pill is reported to have been widely tested in both Europe and the third world, but the Medical Director of Roussell in Britain has said that the drug is only in early clinical development and much further study is needed. It does not take much imagination to predict the future if this pill becomes as easily available as the contraceptive pill. People are all different, and most drugs produce side effects. Where a woman wishes to keep an abortion secret, she could end up with medical complications for which she would then be loth to seek treatment. The long-term effects as yet are unknown. This could be a lethal way out, for mother as well as baby, more dangerous because it is more easily performed.

In the fourth and fifth methods mentioned above, the Infant Preservation Act of 1929 is being flouted, making these abortions illegal. This Act makes it an offence for any person to destroy the life of a child 'capable of being born alive' by 'any wilful act' or to cause 'a child to die before it has an existence independent of its mother.'

A public enquiry was carried out after the shocking affair of the Stobhill Hospital baby in Glasgow, when a baby was taken from the theatre after a hysterotomy and put in a disposal bag ready for the incinerator. The hospital porter, about to throw it in, heard the baby cry. He rushed back to the theatre, where the child was resuscitated but survived only a few more hours, due to severe head injuries. At the enquiry, the coroner asked whether a baby born alive should not be resuscitated, but the answer from the pathologist was that that would defeat the purpose of the operation, which was to abort the baby. The conclusion at the enquiry was that everything had been done legally. Yet according to the Infant Preservation Act, it was flouting the law. The 1967 Abortion Act, contrary to general opinion, does *not* permit abortion up to the twenty-eighth week of pregnancy. It actually sets no limits, relying on the 1929 Act to cover late abortions; but in practice, this is not working to save babies.

Since my twin babies slowly tightened their hold on life over thirty years ago, there has been much progress in neonatal knowledge and care. The 1929 Act allowed late terminations of pregnancy *only* to preserve the life of the mother. With the advances in obstetrics and gynaecology, this reason accounts now for only five annual abortions after twenty-four weeks of pregnancy. The rest then, are performed purely for 'social' reasons and are technically illegal, as well as immoral.

In 1984 *The Lancet* published an article by P.M. Dunn and G.M. Stirrat of Bristol Maternity Hospital, entitled 'Capable of being Born Alive', in which they stated that approximately half of the babies registered as 'liveborn' *before* twenty-eight weeks gestation age could survive to go home to their parents. Even the Short Report, approving eugenic ('for the good of the race' – what a misnomer!) non-treatment of new born handicapped babies, admitted that even in small premature babies cerebral haemorrhage and respiratory failure could be overcome 'with optimum care before, during and after delivery'. Why, then, is this 'optimum care' not given to the victims of hysterotomy, when there are not enough babies to go round for adoption in this country?

There is no practical difference between a hysterotomy and a premature caesarean section, yet one baby is incinerated, while another is given 'optimum care'. It is all a matter of choice. Whose choice? There may be pressure, from doctor, parents, partner or anyone else, but the ultimate choice, since the 1967 Act, is the mother's. She is the person who ultimately decides whether her baby lives or dies.

As a society, we have corporately, since 1967, decided that a mother has that right to choose – the power of life or death over another human being. But as a Church, as individual Christians, we need to ask ourselves what the criterion should be and whether any person has the right to make such a choice. Increasingly, the Christian conscience in this country has been troubled. Many arguments in support of the Act have proved, with time, to be invalid. Pro-abortionists claimed that the Act would abolish backstreet abortionists; that it would stop child abuse because every child would be a wanted child; that it would cement family relationships. All of this has been disproved statistically.

In other countries where abortion has been legalised there has been no reduction in backstreet abortion, or illegal abortions (those performed by unqualified practitioners). Before our 1967 Act, those in its favour argued that there would be less health risk or death arising if the practice was legalised. The facts are that our hospitals are still treating as many cases as before, with problems arising from abortion performed by unqualified people as well as those with complications after NHS abortions. There will always be a demand for the private operator because women will always desire to keep some pregnancies secret, whether women having affairs unknown to their husbands, women in the public eye known to local hospital and medical staff, or unmarried girls not wishing their parents to know.

Obviously backstreet abortions which do not need subsequent hospital treatment are not recorded, so the actual abortion figures could be quite considerably higher than those quoted.

The Act has fostered a less responsible attitude to contraception so that some women even regard abortion as a form of birth control. While contraception, as its name suggests, stops the conception of a child, abortion destroys the child after fertilisation. When we contemplate the truly staggering wonder of the programming which fertilisation starts, the distinction becomes even more significant. Abortion is *not* birth control or family planning. It is legalised killing.

A report in the *Nursing Times* in 1971 told how Rumania had tightened back its laws rigidly, after noting the problems of abortion on demand: 'The result was no increase in backstreet abortion for the first time and an increased respect for women.' It is interesting to note that other countries have also tightened up legislation, where abortion on demand has been in operation longer than we have had it in Britain.

What about respect for children? Albert Schweitzer held that if a man loses reverence for any part of life, he will lose reverence for all life. There are those who argued that if every child was wanted there would be no baby- or child-battering. But even before the Act, statistics from Aberdeen refuted this. Due to an unusual law which did not affect the rest of Scotland, abortion in that city had been legal for over thirty years, so ideally the record for child abuse there should have been different. Aberdeen, conversely, had an unusually high record for abused, uncared for and abandoned children, compared with the rest of Scotland. Those working with, or assessing, child abuse figures will confirm that even wanted babies become cruelty statistics. There is no tie-up with the mother's pre-natal feelings.

In most countries where abortion legislation is liberal, child abuse is on the increase. Since 1967, Britain has also shown an increase in child abuse. Latest figures show that in 1984, 50,000 children were physically and mentally abused, neglected and emotionally starved. Caroline Moorhead in *The Times* (18 December 1984) quoted an officer of the British section of the Save the Children Fund as saying, 'Over the last ten years, the position for all children, has got worse. Children simply count for less in British society than they did.'

Accepting that a human being can be disposed of by another person's choice inevitably leads to an uncaring attitude to all life, especially the old, the ill, the young, the physically handicapped and mentally subnormal. We can see all of these attitudes gaining prevalence in our society, with increasing debate about euthanasia and whether there is a life 'worth living' in some situations. There is a sinister tendency for life today to be assessed on its cost-effectiveness.

Any society which kills its weaker members rather than caring for them is perpetuating the kind of philosophy which shocked the world at Auschwitz and Dachau. Hitler killed the unborn, the physically and mentally handicapped, the old, the sick and those who were doctrinally opposed to his regime. St Paul says (1 Corinthians 1.27), 'God chose the weak things of the world to *shame* the strong.'

Christ came into our world, through pre-natal existence, and was born into a family. He taught that when we put God's laws first, the sick are healed, the hungry are fed, the weak are made strong, those who 'have' share with those who 'have not'. He urged us to beware of those who kill the body but are not able to kill the soul. Each of us is a unique human being with a part of us (the spirit or soul) which

19

responds to God. That alone should arouse a natural pro-Life urge within us. As Christians, we believe that God has a purpose for each life on earth, whether we thwart his plan for us or not. Human lives are being prematurely destroyed and God's plans thwarted by human intervention. For all we know, we could have put back a cure for cancer by aborting a future researcher, delayed world peace by terminating the life of a future great statesman. (Alternatively, we could have destroyed another little Hitler because not all babies born will follow God's will for their lives.)

Abortion is not by any means a hundred per cent safe, even in National Health Service hospitals. There are physical as well as psychological repercussions, even after so-called safe legal abortions. In the first ten years after the Act, seventy-two out of the eighty-six deaths recorded as the result of an abortion were NHS patients. The *British Medical Journal*, 18 August 1978, puts this down to lack of skill in performing the operation, in anaesthetising or in treating complications arising. In the private sector statistics cannot be correctly assessed, since private operators are not required to inform the patient's own doctor. (This is dangerous, because it may affect a further pregnancy.) Deaths from complications discovered later are therefore recorded under the actual cause of death, e.g. sepsis, haemorrhage, embolism, brain damage.

The 1974 Lane Report of the Committee of Enquiry into the working of the Abortion Act said: 'Moreover, the number of deaths from abortion of all kinds in England and Wales is as high now as it was before the Act. Any decrease in the number of deaths from criminal abortion is matched by a rise in the number of deaths from induced abortion.'

The *British Medical Journal* of 29 May 1976 carried a paper on 'The effects of legal termination on subsequent pregnancy', in which J. Richardson and G. Dixon gave statistics from a survey carried out on pregnant women who had previously had abortions. Over 43 per cent had become pregnant again within a year of a termination. (This tendency was also noted by the house-mother of a LIFE house (see in chapter 11). The loss of the second baby before birth was 17.5 per cent compared to 7.5 per cent in women who had had previous spontaneous abortions (i.e. miscarriages). There was also a greater number of premature babies: 13.7 per cent compared to 5.2 per cent after a miscarriage. Over half of the mothers who had had abortions had given birth to subsequent babies between the thirty-seventh and fortieth week of pregnancy and only 21.8 per cent after forty weeks. The rate for perinatal and neonatal death of babies was also higher.

If a woman has had an abortion, and wants to have a baby later, it is imperative that she should inform her gynaecologist, if details are not already on her medical notes. Damage to the cervix or puncture of the womb can lead to problems which a doctor cannot remedy if he is ignorant of past medical details.

All of this aftermath seems a high price to pay for a woman to choose to have a baby just when she wants to have it, even when she has knowingly conceived a child. It is also a high price for our nation to turn away from the reverence and sanctity of life for the sake of expediency or cost-effectiveness, quite apart from the fact that abortion and its consequences bring heavy financial costs.

But who pays the highest price? Obviously, the baby, in pain and loss of life, for it is a fallacy to imply that the baby does not feel pain. Professor Sir Albert William Liley, called the Father of Foetology because of his outstanding work in this field, says in *The Tiniest Humans*:

There is no biochemical or physiological test we can do to tell that *anyone* is in pain, a phenomenon which makes it very easy to bear other people's pain stoically, which is an important point for obstetricians to remember . . . I can only tell you that the foetus responds violently to stimuli which you and I would find painful, e.g. needle puncture, and injection of cold and hypertonic solution.

Senior obstetricians and gynaecologists have also confirmed that the foetus moves away from a needle or other stimuli, and therefore has to be sedated through sedating the mother, before intra-uterine treatment. It does feel pain; increased movement and heartbeat confirm this.

As if this were not enough it is also agonising for Christians of conscience to see the lengths to which medical science is going in experimentation on live results of late abortions, or on babies fertilised in a test-tube and 'grown up' for research. While most Christians would wholeheartedly support any ethical form of help for childless couples, the 'spare' embryos grown only for experimentation are a different matter.

Legislation, medical practice, scientific research all bring repercussions for people: people like you and me. People have to accept, adapt and cope with physical and psychological changes or make a stand for the alternatives.

Later in this book I give examples of people who are or have been affected by abortion and its aftermath, or have been misled by fallacies taught about it. Any one of these experiences could have been yours or mine, yet many of us are unaware of what is going on in the legal, medical and scientific world, of the pain to unborn babies and the devastation in some families. Other people quoted have coped and overcome the difficulties. All of them feel strongly about current trends, medical ethics and the alternatives for the future.

3

Whose Body?

The greatest fallacy put about by the pro-abortion lobby is the slogan: 'As a woman, I can do what I like with my own body.'

The same argument is used by smokers, drug addicts and alcoholics. In these cases there is the counter-argument that everything we do affects somebody else, and that victims of their own habits, or over-indulgences, store up pain and problems for their relatives, friends, medical advisers and those caring for them.

The case of a pregnant woman, however, is completely different for she is not talking about her own body, but about someone else's. Once a baby has been conceived, that child is a separate person. Pro-abortionists would have us believe that the baby is not a human being at conception, yet are unable to tell us what it is. If it is not *homo sapiens*, it is definitely not any other species of animal or plant life. It is living, yet it is not a part of the mother's body, because it was not there before conception, nor will it remain there indefinitely, even if it is not aborted.

Professor Jerome Lejeune, in *The Tiniest Humans*, confirms that 'the term "human being" is a scientific definition of a conceptus'. Sir Albert Liley (quoted in the same book) asks, 'If there is nothing there, then why the unholy rush to get rid of it?' Those who consider the conceptus to be merely a 'blob of jelly' are ignoring the scientific facts.

What is the medical and scientific proof that life begins at conception when the female egg is fertilised by the male sperm?

Professor Hymie Gordon, Chairman of the Department of Medical Genetics in the Mayo Clinic, reported to a Congressional Hearing in April 1981, with regard to abortion:

> From the moment of conception, the organism contains many complex molecules; it synthesises new intricate structures from simple raw materials and it replicates itself. By all the criteria of modern molecular biology, life is present from the moment of conception.

Dr Watson A. Bowes of the University of Colorado Medical School said:

> Following fertilisation there is an inexorable series of events that unfolds, with cells dividing, moving, pausing, differentiating and aggregating with a baffling precision and purpose. In the early hours, days and weeks of this development, a hypothetical observer, if able to witness this microscopic drama, would find it impossible to identify precisely when major qualitative changes have occurred, just as parents, observing daily their child's growth and development, cannot say precisely when he or she stopped being a child and became an adult . . . Thus the beginning of a single human life is from a biological point of view a simple straightforward matter – the beginning is conception. This is a straightforward biological fact and should not be distorted to serve sociological, political or economic goals.

In Britain, the work of Drs Steptoe and Edwards in test-tube baby research, the growing up of babies *in vitro* (i.e. 'in glass', in a test-tube, outside the womb) accentuates the fact that from the beginning the fertilised single cell is a separate entity. It receives the egg from the mother's

24

body, an egg which otherwise would have been discarded by that body, and which is therefore not an integral part of it, rather the half of a whole new life – only able to come to its full potential when in union with the other half of it, the father's contribution to the embryo. Then the miracle happens. On a slender coiled thread, that can be balanced on a pinpoint, the genetic information of the new baby is stored. The size of feet, colour of hair and eyes, length of fingers etc. is already determined.

The first single-celled conceptus is not just the blueprint of a baby. A blueprint is only a plan: it does not contain the power to put that plan into completion. This powerful new human cell has the capacity, inbuilt, to develop and grow by way of its own perfect programming. The 30,000,000,000,000 cells that make up your adult body have evolved because that first cell doubled, divided, doubled each division and repeated this growth process until the forty-fifth time. After your first journey, from your mother's fallopian tube to her womb, when, gestationally, you were six or eight days old, eight of these divisions had been made.

Your mother was two months pregnant, perhaps only just realising it, by the time thirty growth divisions had occurred. The next nine took five more months (a time when babies are still being aborted). Two more happened in the last two months before you were born. The last four longer growth processes took up the whole of your childhood and adolescence.

Your mother's body gave you warmth, protection and food. This in itself is another miracle of nature. Today we hear a great deal about transplant surgery. It is well known that one body will reject the tissue of another. However, we do not have to tissue type our parents. The baby is 'foreign' to its mother in an immunological sense, yet the baby solves what is called the homograft problem. The mother and baby have to tolerate each other's tissues while

25

nourishment, etc. is passed between them. Sir Albert Liley comments that this problem, which so far has defeated the best brains in surgery and immunology, was solved by you and by me before we were born, or we would not be here today. A Nobel Prize awaits the person who can remember how he did it!

Once implanted into the sponge-like lining of the womb, the conceptus develops a placenta and a sac (or capsule) of fluid for himself. The mother's body does not provide either of these, only the nutrients which are passed to the baby through the placenta.

It seems incredible that you, as a microscopic embryo, were able not only to programme your own development and environment but also to produce substances to prolong the normal life of the womb lining, preventing it from being shed. You took over your mother's womb and its functions, stopped her menstrual cycle, solved that homograft problem of your tissue working with hers, and determined your own birthday (unless you had medical intervention). If you are an identical twin, you were even able to phenocopy yourself asexually. The amniotic fluid in which you swam was yours. If it was tested, the tests were tests on you, not on your mother. When it was dispensed with, it was you who started off the process (again unless doctors intervened).

Your heart was formed and beating twenty-five days after you were conceived. Five days later, when you were only about a quarter of an inch long, your brain was of human proportions, you had eyes, mouth, ears, kidney, liver and an umbilical cord. Your heart was pumping blood made by your own body. By your forty-fifth day, your skeleton was complete in cartilage, you had the buds of your milk teeth and could move your newly grown limbs, yet still your mother barely knew that she carried you.

At sixteen weeks you were half your birth length.

At twenty weeks you weighed about a pound, measured about a foot, and your hair began to appear.

At twenty-eight weeks you opened your eyes. You could hear your mother's digestive processes and her heartbeat and even a door being banged loudly, or noisy music!

This is a laywoman's simplification of a process which, when studied, staggers the scientist. The inbuilt techniques are so awe-inspiring that many researchers have come over to the pro-Life camp.

Do you consider that in the womb you were a part of your mother's body? Of course you do not. You were a unique, new, living miracle. God had never created a replica of you before and he never will again. As the Psalmist says, you were 'fearfully and wonderfully made,' as has been every baby, even those we call handicapped.

But familiarity has bred contempt. We take our bodily functions and capabilities so much for granted, that until some life-or-death trauma enters our lives, we expect nature to keep working for us. We complain when small things go wrong, instead of thanking our Creator every day that they go right. If we slightly hurt one small part of our bodies, we soon realise just how much each part relies on the next. Yet at some time in the lives of most of us, we are faced with a serious accident or illness. Death suddenly shatters our family peace and happiness. At the root of all our knowledge at such times is the awareness that, in reality, that slender thread we call life is beyond our power to create, to sustain or to destroy legitimately. We are forced even if reluctantly to own the sovereign power of a Creator.

For some women or young girls who have an abortion, this facing up to life may not yet have happened. From childhood, they have taken life and health for granted. They have been taught to trust the professionals unquestioningly, to accept the superior medical knowledge of the general practitioner or consultant. It is often only at a much

27

later date that the full significance of what they have destroyed hits them.

My own body?

4

The Guilt and Grief of Abortion

The personal aftermath of abortion is the mixture of grief and guilt that arises directly afterwards, or sometimes after an interval of months or even years.

Grief is natural and only time can heal that. However, family and friends do need to recognise that grief will occur.

Guilt is different. How is it expiated?

Japan has an exorbitant abortion rate, with the average woman having several. This may appal us, but it does not stop there. Keeping pace with the abortion rate, there are temples filling up with row upon row of wooden dolls. Women can buy wooden dolls of differing prices (to suit differing weights of guilt?), often straining the pocket. Clothes in which to dress the dolls are also offered in varying price ranges. The doll is placed in the temple in memory of the aborted baby. On the anniversary of the baby's termination, gifts of flowers or fruit are placed before the doll. Japanese women say this helps them to get over the trauma of abortion. They are also helped to remember the child they would have had. The sight of such temples, filled with wooden dolls in memory of babies sacrificed on the altar of expediency, was sickening to many British women when it was depicted on our TV screens in 1983. Playing on the guilt and grief of women after abortion, commercialising its expiation, is obviously a growing business with lucrative results for the 'priests' of the temples.

After the film was screened, a selection of British women who had had abortions were asked what they thought of the idea. Some thought it was good. It would have helped them with the guilt they all felt, and they 'would have got over it quicker' (I wonder!). So, apparently, it could happen here.

How far can we go in this hypocritical attitude to abortion? Forgiveness, and release from guilt, personal or corporate, cannot be obtained by token offerings of and to wooden dolls. Human guilt has been dealt with once and for all by the only expert on the subject, God who created us. As Christians we believe that only in the sacrifice of Christ on the cross at Calvary can we know complete forgiveness, healing and therapy for all our guilt and fears. If you have had an abortion, buying and dressing a wooden doll, and making an annual oblation of flowers or fruit, will not erase the pain of that experience. When we are bruised we need love. No human love can help our deepest hurts, only in the infinite sacrificial love of God himself in Jesus can we find comfort and healing, as well as forgiveness and strength for the future. To own our need of that love and forgiveness is to know it. That is the only way to achieve real peace of mind. This is borne out by Noreen Riols, whose book *Eye of the Storm*, described how she herself had an abortion. She wrote to me:

If only I had known then what I know now!

I wonder how many other women have echoed these words which have sprung to my lips so many times since that day in 1967 when I woke up in a hospital bed and realised that it was all over. The child which had been growing in my body for the last three months was no longer there: he or she had been removed, 'aborted for medical reasons.'

I was forty at the time and we already had five children but, even so, I carried not only the pain but the guilt of that abortion with me for a very long time, knowing that I was the one who had consigned my unborn baby to a nameless grave, maybe

30

even the hospital incinerator and, after listening to a lot of good, perfectly reasonable and well-meant advice, had decided that it was the only thing to do.

But was it?

Somewhere I had read: 'Take what you want,' God says, 'and pay for it.'

And that, in effect, is what God *does* say. He gives us free will to choose between right and wrong, as he had given me that morning when I signed the operation consent form; but in return, we pay for our choice.

And I paid.

For months afterwards it seemed that everywhere I looked a finger was pointing accusingly at me. If I turned on the radio there was a discussion on abortion with opinions offered as to whether the unborn baby suffered. Every magazine I picked up seemed to fall open at the picture of a three-month-old foetus with a description of how it was extracted from the womb.

Over and over again I woke in the night telling myself that I had had no choice; but deep down I knew that I had had a choice: that no one could have taken that baby from me without my consent. And, for a long time, nothing could wipe out the dreadful guilt I felt knowing that I had agreed to the murder of my own child, and I was unable to forgive myself for what I had done.

Yet it was through the pain and depression I experienced that I stopped being just a churchgoer and came to know Jesus as my personal Saviour. He was the only one to whom I could talk without hearing platitudes, the only one who was able to take away my guilt and from whom I was finally able to receive the forgiveness I was seeking.

Through this encounter with the living Lord I was born again into the new life Jesus promises to all who come to him and receive his gift: and when that happened, I was liberated from my pain and guilt.

I think I knew before I had the abortion that what I was

about to consent to was wrong. Doesn't the Bible say that even if we have never heard of God – and I had heard of him in church every Sunday from my earliest childhood – we all instinctively know right from wrong? And, instinctively, even though so many good, kind, well-meaning and competent people had advised me that to have another child would be a disaster, somewhere in my muddled thinking of the time, I knew that I was going against the natural law and against the law of God.

But I was afraid. Afraid of what another baby might do to me. I had had a bad puerperal depression after the birth of the last one and had twice been in a psychiatric clinic and, when I became pregnant again, not then knowing Jesus personally, I had relied on my own feelings – which are usually misleading – and other people's advice. And the doctors told me that another baby would probably cost me my sanity.

Had I known Jesus as I know him now, when I was stumbling blindly through that dark valley, I would have placed myself and my unborn child in his hands and said, 'Lord, the decision is yours.'

And I know what his decision would have been. I would now have a son or daughter coming of age this year.

I am sure many women suffer as I did, often in silence and bitterness, not only the terrible pangs of indecision – that awful limbo between the longing to hold a baby in their arms and the fear, either materialistic, or medical or even social, of what that baby might do to them and their family. And I am sure that 'reason' often wins and, as abortion on demand becomes more and more of a reality, many more women are going to suffer the aftermath.

Peer pressure and the desire to conform are difficult to ignore, especially for the young and those who, without Jesus to turn to, are going to be pressurised into this 'modern, reasonable' solution.

In 1967 when I made my decision, medical abortions had only just become legal and 'social abortions' were still a backstreet affair. And I had time to think before I acted. But how much more difficult it is for the women of the eighties when instant abortion for almost any reason is the order of the day. How many of them will be rushed into taking a decision which, like me, they may well regret for the rest of their lives?

I know the inevitable question of handicapped children will be raised. But I cannot help thinking about Mary Craig's moving book, *Blessings* and what she had to say about her two handicapped boys; what it taught them all as a family to have a son and a brother who was not like everyone else; how much it showed them of the real meaning of love; and how much love these 'different' children showered on them in return.

She did not have the option of an abortion, but I remember hearing her speak on a radio programme dealing with this delicate subject when she was asked what would have happened had she had the option. She had shuddered at the thought, saying that all their lives had been enriched by these two boys whose brains would always remain those of innocent children.

And hers is not the only testimony of this kind. She was not given the choice; but I heard a very moving witness recently from a young married couple who had been. They are in their twenties and were thrilled and excited when they learned that they were to become parents. But the bubble of joy was soon to be deflated when the doctors told them that there was a grave risk of the baby being born handicapped and strongly advised an abortion. They reeled at the idea and were hardly able to grasp what was being said to them: but shortly afterwards they returned to the hospital with their decision. 'We are committed Christians,' they told the doctors calmly, 'and believe that every child is a gift from God and, as such, we will accept and love whatever baby the Lord gives us.'

I do not know what the medical reaction was, or what the hospital team had to say in private, but I do know that although doctors are dedicated people advising only what they think is right, they are not infallible: and that young couple now have a beautiful, healthy, perfectly normal baby daughter.

I wonder how many other babies have been denied life because of the grave risks attached to the possibility of their not being born perfect.

Two of our friends had 'mistakes' at the same time as we did. Those 'mistakes' are coming up to their eighteenth birthdays. As I have watched these two children at all stages of their development, each new stage as they grew to adulthood has brought a pang to my heart knowing that I, too, could have had that joy and fulfilment which has been their parents' as they guided them through to maturity.

They had both seemed like disasters at the time they were conceived, coming when their parents thought their pattern of family life was now established and they had finished with nappies. Yet not long ago we were discussing abortion and the Warnock Report and the father of one of these 'mistakes' said:

'Jenny was a catastrophe, or at least when we knew she was on the way we thought she was. The other three were already in school, I had just launched out in a new business, money was at its tightest and the idea of another mouth to feed overwhelmed us. Perhaps, had the abortion laws been then as they are now, we would have been very tempted, as all reason and good sense were against our bringing another child into the world.'

He suddenly shivered, put his arm around his wife who was sitting beside him and said to her: 'Just think, if we'd had the choice, there might have been no Jenny. I can't imagine life without her, can you? She's been a blessing to us all.'

His wife nodded and added, 'How terrible for couples today to be *given* the choice.'

Theirs would have been an abortion for convenience, or for economic reasons because, materially, it had not at that time seemed possible to stretch their over-burdened budget to include another child. But they had managed to!

Mine had been for medical or mental health reasons. And yet, looking back, we both felt the same way. I had made the wrong decision and they were thankful they had not been tempted to do so.

I have heard so many say the same thing, and wept with those who have afterwards regretted what they have done; for I now realise that peace of mind depends not on the economy or our material well-being, or even the absence of danger or difficulties in our lives, but on the presence of Jesus.

And didn't God say; 'I have set before you life and death . . . Now choose life, so that you and your children may live' (Deuteronomy 30.19).

Do we need any further guidance?

Guilt and grief are always curiously interwoven, often indistinguishable. In this state, we are very vulnerable. After any bereavement, we feel guilty, as well as sad, asking ourselves whether we did all we could for the lost loved one.

Lynne and Pete are a young couple who had a harrowing experience. They are visibly upset when they hear the word 'abortion'. Their story illustrates the pain that infertile couples are going through at this time of liberal abortion.

For three years they tried to have a baby, not seeking medical help because they both feared that the doctors would tell them that parenthood was impossible for them. Eventually, they knew they had to find out and were directed to the clinic to try AIH (artificial insemination by the husband). Then began the long process of Lynne taking her temperature every day to find out her most fertile time, for Pete to rush to the clinic at that time and for Lynne to be artifically inseminated by her husband. Every month there was hope and then disappointment, but for three years this couple persevered because of their longing for their own child.

The wonderful day came. Lynne had a pregnancy test and learned the result as early as the sixteenth day. She was going to have the child for which they had waited six years.

Their joy did not last long. At three months when she had a scan, Lynne was told to rest, then come back for another. She knew she was ill and that something was wrong. The amniotic sac burst and the fluid left her. She went to bed and did all she was told, but her stomach swelled up as if she were full-term pregnant and she felt terrible. After two weeks when she went back to the hospital for the second scan, she was told that there was abnormal placental growth and that the baby would have to be taken from her, but it would die anyway. If the operation were delayed, she might jeopardise her chances of having another child. Both Lynne and Pete knew they had no choice, but Lynne was haunted by the thought of abortion. Unfortunately, the medical term for a miscarriage such as Lynne experienced is 'spontaneous abortion', and as she is totally against deliberate termination of pregnancy, she was extremely hurt when a young doctor asked her, 'Is this your first abortion?'

Lynne says she knew that when she went into that hospital her baby was alive, but after the operation it had gone. She still feels guilty.

Afterwards, she was not at all well. She tried to fight her tiredness and lack of energy. She bled on and off for fourteen weeks – maybe nature's way of cleaning out her womb thoroughly, but she felt ill. She was weak and drained.

After three months she went back to the clinic to start the long process all over again. Other mothers visited the clinic for antenatal checks. When Lynne heard them complaining about having to see the doctor or having to make another hospital appointment, she felt very angry. She wanted to tell them how fortunate they were to be pregnant and to be well looked after. She and Pete have nothing but praise for the staff of that clinic, their doctor and gynaecologist, who helped them through with care, advice and laughter.

Month after month the hopes and disappointments went

on. Each time it was harder to take.

'I felt like throwing that thermometer through the window,' said Lynne. 'It was awful: taking the fertility drug yet still being infertile; taking my temperature and knowing the 'right' time, yet it never was; and having some people telling us to forget about it until we could have a baby 'properly'. Because we knew that there were problems on both sides, it made it easier. Before we both had tests, we each used to blame ourselves and feel guilty because we could not give each other a child. We were trying so hard, but because it was AIH people thought it was wrong, and that hurt us. We couldn't see that it was wrong when only the two of us were involved. I would have done anything to have a baby, even a test-tube baby, but there's no chance here, only in London and it's so expensive. I would have raised the money somehow if I knew it would work first time, but it doesn't always, does it? Then we would have been even more upset.'

Pete told me: 'When we first went to the clinic, we thought we were different, but we were amazed at how many people there are who can't have babies (one in eight couples in Britain today). When you walk down the High Street there are prams and children everywhere. You think you are the only childless ones around. It helped to know that others were going through the same experience and we could talk to someone who understood.'

In the thirteenth month of the second long wait to conceive, Lynne knew that this time it was positive again.

'All the signs pointed to my being pregnant. I had a test, but could not believe the answer. It was confirmed and my doctor took special care of me. I couldn't have had better treatment anywhere.'

Pete laughed: 'She didn't lift anything heavier than a duster for the whole time. I took over the housework and shopping, washing and ironing.'

'It's surprising how quickly the time went considering I

did practically nothing at all,' Lynne said. 'The first bit was the worst: getting over the first three months, the stage at which I'd lost my first baby. The next worry was that I didn't feel him move until I was five months pregnant and everyone was telling me I'd know he was all right because I could feel him at four and a half months. I suppose two more weeks wouldn't make any difference to most women, but I still couldn't believe that things would go right. Suddenly, at seven months, I really felt fit, and wanted to go out. Up to then it had been discomfort all the way, but at the time when most women are feeling big, awkward and tired, I took on a new lease of life and felt on top of the world. I was only just letting myself believe that I was actually pregnant and everything was going fine.

'It was a difficult birth. They said that I might have to have a caesarean section, but I wanted to have my baby naturally. I wanted to show them I could do something all on my own. Pete was there all the time and kept me going. Even at the end, when they had to drug me for the pain, he was wringing out wet cloths and putting them on my forehead to keep me awake, as I was determined not to miss it. The pillow was soaked and the staff laughed and said he'd almost drowned me.

'Although I had a lot of stitches, our baby was born naturally. It was indescribable to have him at last.'

'When they put him in my arms after all that, it was unbelievable,' Pete admitted.

Lynne went on: 'But I'll never forget that I was pregnant before. It was our baby, even though we had to do what we did. We'll always remember . . . It was terrible afterwards. Having a baby now doesn't mean that he's taken the place of the one we lost. We know that once before, we gave life to a child . . .'

Lynne and Pete have a beautiful child and yet are still haunted by that first 'abortion'. Their grief and guilt had to be worked through, even though there was a valid medical reason for what happened. Their story shows the pain of childless parents who see others wantonly discarding their babies. Like Noreen, these parents have countless times wanted to shout out at more fortunate parents: 'Choose life, so that you and your children may live.'

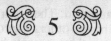

5

Fathers

The unfair legal position of the father compounds the fallacy that the baby is part of a woman's own body.

At the moment of conception, the baby's father contributes to the child equally with the mother a genetic bank of information which, when joined to hers, sets in action the future programming of his unique son or daughter. While it is true that God has not chosen the father's body to be the incubator and food supply, he did set us in families. The father has a moral right to a knowledge of and share in his child's progress and future. That progress and future start at conception, not at birth, yet a father has no legal right to prevent his wife's or girlfriend's abortion. Christian and pro-Life family doctors can thus find themselves faced with the moral dilemma of divided loyalty. Does the wife or husband win? Legally, at present, the woman.

The upsurge of the women's liberation movement, the advent of the contraceptive pill and the Abortion Act have all given strength to the feminist voice. (Having said that, not all feminists are for abortion. For instance, Women for Life gives an education and advisory service and fights against abortion.)

All of the old arguments and illustrations of male dominance and sexual arrogance have been aired. It is in this climate that the 'I can do what I like with my own body' doctrine was born.

It is of course not difficult to find cases of men abusing women, many of whom are shamefully abandoned once they are pregnant. The structure of our society seems weighted to the advantage of such uncaring men. Unmarried women and their babies have access to help and accommodation, enabling the men responsible to go free with no pressure to provide homes or moral support. Women opting for abortion frequently go through the trauma of decision deserted by boyfriend or co-habitor, sometimes by a husband; but there is always the other side of the coin. Many conscientious and caring men have gone through agonies knowing that their child has been destroyed and there has been nothing that can reverse that act. In Maryland, a man took his wife to court to try to stop her having an abortion. He lost the case.

The time factor for the decision means that an abortion can be over before the father finds out that he is going to have a child. If he does find out, pressure from a single girl's parents or the woman's doctor, plus sometimes a natural animosity from the person he has landed 'in trouble', often gives him no chance to discuss the matter.

If he is married and his wife wants to hide her pregnancy and abortion, his doctor has no legal right to tell him. The doctor's loyalty is to his patient, to the wife. He has to respect her privacy. Can this be morally or ethically right? Are the pro-Life agencies doing anything at all for such men?

Most men are thrilled at the thought of becoming fathers. It is not only a question of having proved their manhood or the prospect of buying a train set at Christmas. Underneath the British stiff upper lip tradition men experience much more pleasure, and pain, from their family relationships than we usually credit them with. Every family has its share of trauma, and men often suffer in silence because they feel their close relatives are relying on them to be strong. Today's men are experiencing real grief and shock after abortion.

I followed the stories of three men; one unmarried, one

41

facing the prospect of losing his first child, the third married with other children.

A counsellor of a LIFE group, without breaking any confidences, told me that she has often received telephone calls from men in tears because their babies were to be aborted. One call still haunts that counsellor.

The man had been living with a woman separated from her husband. She was pleased when she became pregnant, because she had left her other children, but during the pregnancy her husband contacted her, asking her to return to the family home and try again to make the marriage work. She agreed, but had to own up about the coming baby, whereupon her husband refused to take her back unless she had an abortion. She accepted his condition. The baby's father, doubly upset at losing her and his child, tried to persuade her to keep the baby, which he planned to bring up himself with the help of his family. But the legal husband refused to allow his wife to carry on with the pregnancy and the child was aborted. The LIFE counsellor, while believing it right for the wife to return to her husband and children, was nevertheless deeply concerned about the father's distress, as also about the loss of the baby.

Laxity of sexual morals, and the increasing break-up of homes and families, cause pain and problems all round. The victims of this new code of behaviour are countless. The casual attitude to sex, the decreasing value to society of life in the womb, is a symptom of our 'disposable' age. Just as we throw away all else for which we have no further use, we are disposing of people, especially unborn people. That mother had been looking forward to the birth of her child, yet as soon as the husband offered to have her back, her new partner and his coming child were disposed of. The man has learned to his high cost the price of casual relationships, and he may have lost the only child he will ever father.

42

Arthur Shostak, an American sociologist, interviewed a thousand men whose babies had been aborted. He believes that abortion is a great unrecognised trauma that men have to endure silently, without help. He spent ten years studying the subject after experiencing totally unexpected grief and shock when the child of his former lover was aborted, and he urges the need for some sort of support group for these men. His findings were used for his book, *Men and Abortion: Lessons and Love.*

Is the prospect for fathers then completely negative?

One father I interviewed managed to save his daughter's life, although it cost him his marriage.

I visited Richard and Helen just after Christmas. Helen, then aged eight, had been rehearsing for her part in the local pantomime. She is a lively, intelligent child, obviously happy. Richard, a teacher, was forty-three when his wife, a nursing sister, became pregnant. They had married later than some, so this was their first child. His wife arranged to have an abortion without Richard's knowledge, but fortunately for Helen, he found out before it took place. Looking back, he believes that God guided him through those next few days, when anger and fear that the abortion might go through drove him to do everything in his power to stop it.

First, Richard telephoned the hospital to find out the name of the gynaecologist. He knew he would not get an appointment to see him through his general practitioner, since it was the GP who had referred the wife for abortion, so Richard went to the hospital and waylaid the consultant. Having agreed to talk, the consultant asked that two other members of staff be present at the interview. When they met, Richard asked whether the gynaecologist had any children. He had four, he said. Richard then pointed out that the child he was about to kill would probably be *his* only one, considering the ages of himself and his wife. He

43

threatened to go to the law, the press, the media and to his Member of Parliament if the abortion was not stopped. The consultant, who confessed he had never been in such a position before, said he would have to consult the Medical Defence Union.

Richard left the hospital still a very worried man, and praying that the termination would not be performed.

'I knew no solicitor in this town,' he told me, 'yet, even in my distress, I was guided straight to a sympathetic one, who acted immediately to help me. Knowing current thinking among some solicitors, I am still amazed at that.'

Letters were drafted to the GP and the consultant, and sent by personal messenger to save time. Richard also contacted the local Roman Catholic priest, whose church his wife attended.

The GP and the gynaecologist obviously realised that this father would go to any lengths to save his child. The priest talked to the mother. The abortion was called off.

When Helen was born, Richard still hoped that he could save his marriage and enjoy a normal family life with his wife and daughter. But Helen's mother was still unwilling to accept motherhood. She stayed a further six weeks in the house, living apart from her husband, until she found alternative accommodation.

Richard claims he made his first mistake when, believing, as he had been advised, that it would be in Helen's best interests, he allowed her to be fostered at six weeks old. There were three sets of foster-parents before the child was three, the second couple wanting to adopt her. Terrified that he would lose her, Richard determined to go all out to have her back with him. He gave up teaching and returned to his former occupation, engraving, which he could do from home.

Richard had a tough fight assuring the social services that he was capable of looking after a young child. At one stage the Salvation Army took up his case. Eventually, he was able to have his daughter home on a permanent basis. He fits in his work from home and cares for Helen, his home and the other member of the family, a lively young dog, an ideal companion for this energetic little girl who so easily could have been just one more abortion statistic. Their new family doctor is a Roman Catholic lady, very sympathetic to Richard's stand to save his daughter's life, who gives him moral and spiritual backing.

Richard's wife later divorced him, but since he had cared for Helen himself for three years before the custody hearing, he was in a strong position to keep her, especially as his wife had no desire to have her. (Latterly, she did decide she would like to get to know her daughter, and now sees her approximately every two weeks.)

Richard maintains that all that has happened in his past has made him a stronger person and a more committed Christian. He feels that God has helped him all along to do what had to be done. After prayer, the right people have always been there when he needed them. He was sad at the failure of his marriage, but now considers himself to be a happy and fulfilled person. He took his marriage vows seriously and says that he will never re-marry. He concluded his letter arranging our first meeting with these words:

> I believe that the spirit is strengthened and refined through suffering. I think that in my case it actually helped me to appreciate life far more than otherwise would have been the case. There is great wisdom in adversity.

Richard is more than willing to help any other father who finds himself in the same situation, but warns that speed is the first consideration. There is very little time in which to act.

The Christian faith is a great paradox. Christ taught that those who try to hold on selfishly to things will lose them, yet those who give all will gain all. His example at Calvary teaches that the way of suffering is the way to victory, that those who choose the harder path will know the ultimate gain. But how much Christian morality is to be found in medical practice today? For every Christian doctor, there are many more who take the secular stance, while all are caught up in painful dilemmas. One such, based on a true-life case, was shown in the television series *Doctor's Dilemma* in January 1985 and was entitled 'A Web of Deception'.

It portrayed a young man who had married a divorcee with two young daughters. After two years, he was becoming anxious because no baby had been conceived. He wondered whether he could be infertile. However, unknown to him, his wife had become pregnant, and had subsequently had the child aborted, after which her doctor had prescribed the birth control pill. The doctor's dilemma started when the husband visited him confidentially about his suspected infertility, asking him not to tell the wife.

From that invidious position, the doctor had to decide on his course of action. He sent the husband for a test, eventually telling him that it might take a while for his wife to conceive because of the low sperm count it revealed. This further undermined the man's confidence, as he felt that he had not come up to the first husband's performance in giving his wife a child. He felt it was his fault they did not have the son they had casually talked of having. Added to this, he was not enjoying too good a relationship with his two stepdaughters.

Eventually, the doctor told the wife of the husband's concern, breaking his confidence. He had first tried to find out if the wife did intend to have more children, and she thought she might, 'later'. However, she refused to tell her husband herself about the birth control on the grounds that he would be angry and the doctor invited her to come to see him with her husband to discuss the whole issue.

The television programme did not reveal how the real-life case was resolved. However, it did highlight a problem which crops up increasingly in doctors' surgeries these days. How can a general practitioner operate as a true family doctor when there are opposing or conflicting interests within the family?

The television doctor considered it was his duty to try to get a dialogue on the subject between the two partners to save the marriage, although he had had no qualms about aborting the baby, the act on which the marriage would founder anyway if it were revealed. He talked to the husband of the 'possibility' of having a child 'later', all the while knowing the mother's feelings, and also that the abortion could have left her sterile. Was it ethical to abort the first, and maybe last, child of this father without his consent? Without his knowledge, even?

A discussion panel which followed on from the programme included a doctor specialising in women's health problems who felt that the question of fertility should always be discussed with both partners, and a psychologist who considered that the doctor was abusing his power over the two by collusion and deceit.

All this leads us to ask whether the father is getting a fair deal on the abortion issue. Is it right that such an important thing as the life of a baby should depend on the choice of one parent only? Some married men, especially, are strongly opposed to this. If both parents had to present themselves to a doctor to request an abortion, if both had to sign away their baby's life, that might stop some potential fathers from having such a casual attitude to sexual intercourse, that wonderful gift of God.

It ought to be hammered home more emphatically in schools' sex education courses that abortion is *not* a contraceptive. It is interesting that one sex education course for schools, *Living and Growing*, does make the point that life begins at conception. Let us make it clear to all our youngsters that it must not end at abortion.

Church youth clubs and discussion groups should invite pro-Life speakers to put the case against abortion-on-demand to potential mothers and fathers. For too long the Church has sat back and ignored the pain resulting from the aftermath of sexual laxity. It often seems to convey an 'I told you so!' attitude, without offering the healing power of the gospel of Christ, who died to bring peace, dignity and forgiveness to all.

That gospel is logical. The ways of God are to be trusted. This has been proved time and again through the ages.

The same cannot be said of current medical ethics and practice, not to mention counselling.

Robert, a father of three, was almost a father of two! He had a fourteen-year-old daughter and an eleven-year-old son. When it was confirmed that his wife was pregnant for the third time, she panicked. It was a natural first reaction for a woman of thirty-six, her first children almost teenagers. The thought of morning sickness, nappies, broken nights and not being able to participate fully in family activities can be daunting at first. On hearing the result of her pregnancy test, this mother's thoughts and feelings were in turmoil. It was at this stage that it was pointed out to her that for women of her age a pregnancy can be terminated as there is a risk of handicap occurring in babies born to 'older women'. It is extremely demoralising to be fed the line that at thirty-six you are an older woman, that you should be past child-bearing, at least with normal results. This big threat of handicap is currently put to women from their mid-thirties whereas, not so long ago, the age of risk was said to be forty-plus. Robert's wife was told that if she did go ahead with her pregnancy, her progress would have to be carefully monitored.

The prospect facing older women is not just a new round

of broken nights, dirty nappies and a teething baby crying when the eldest is trying to cope with school exams, but endless hospital appointments and scans, maybe culminating in a proposal to terminate because of possible handicap anyway. Is it to be wondered at that so many women in their late thirties and early forties are opting for abortion? Robert's wife can testify that it was pressure all the way.

Two weeks after the confirmation of pregnancy, she was given an appointment to see a gynaecologist. (That seems an infinitely shorter wait than for women with problems needing healing!)

Those two weeks were the longest in Robert's life, when he felt incredibly angry and helpless. He wanted to appeal against the counselling his wife had been given, but every time the couple tried to discuss the situation sensibly, so heightened were their emotions that it always ended up in argument, with each screaming at the other.

'I pointed out that the baby was a part of me,' Robert told me. 'If she rejected it or ejected it, she was rejecting me. A part of you does live on in your children, yet at no time had my opinion been sought. This was the way I saw it and I was devastated by it. Men do have feelings. The thought that if my wife had wanted to keep it a secret from me altogether she could have done so, made me angry and emotional. Under National Health Service practice, she would have even been helped to deceive me.'

As the deadline for the hospital appointment loomed large, sensible dialogue had to be resumed. They started to talk and think more constructively about the prospect of another child. They decided against abortion, and wanted to cancel the appointment, but the wife's GP advised that the visit to the hospital go on as planned, as an ordinary pre-natal check. When she attended, she found she was still treated as if she had not changed her mind, even to the extent of being given a date for the abortion to be performed, and the two necessary signatures were put on her form. When she insisted that she did not after all wish the termination to go ahead, she was reminded that she had agreed to it initially (even though at that time she had not been in a state of mind to think clearly). She returned home in a deep depression and told Robert who, in his own words, 'went spare'.

After seventeen years of happy marriage, outside forces and influences were threatening this couple's ability to think, discuss and plan about a vital issue affecting their family life. The outcome could well have been the break-up of their relationship, with Robert losing his wife and family since divorce-on-demand is as rife as abortion. Fortunately, their love for each other was strong enough to stand the pressure.

Robert recalls: 'Before that appointment, during those two traumatic weeks, I tried everything I could think of. I went to the Citizens' Advice Bureau, and to my solicitor, but no one had any power to help me, legally. Although this affected my wife, my children, my family, the answer was always the same: I had no legal rights to know about the abortion or to stop it. When my wife told her doctor that she was definitely not going to the hospital to have the abortion, she was told that she must cancel the arrangement herself, although she had previously insisted that she did not want an admission date.'

At every stage this mother was being faced with another 'final decision', another chance to be tempted to take abortion as the easy way out. Her medical advisers seemed not to take No for an answer. She did eventually cancel the abortion, and then there began the careful monitoring of her pregnancy, including eight scans and an offer of amniocentesis (a process by which a sample of the amniotic fluid around the baby is drawn off and tested for evidence of possible handicap). This last offer was refused because the risk (one chance in a hundred) of bleeding, and hence of a miscarriage, if the placenta is pierced accidentally, was actually greater than the risk of Robert's wife, merely because of her age, having a defective baby (a one-in-three-hundred chance). It now seems to be general practice to offer amniocentesis to 'older' mothers. It is sometimes argued that this is a good thing; a positive test can be reassuring in circumstances where there has been a previous bad medical history, for instance when a mother has lost a baby or had a badly handicapped child. But Professor Lejeune, the geneticist who discovered the cause of Down's syndrome, is of the opinion that to have the test for purely psychological reasons is not worth the risk. One in a hundred may seem like a remote chance, but if that one is your baby, it is no chance at all.

Robert and his wife now have a beautiful son, physically perfect. When she looks at her child this mother still often bursts into tears at the thought of what might have been his fate. Robert remains angry at the way in which fathers are treated, or rather ignored, on the subject of abortion. He admits to still feeling very emotional when the subject comes up.

Because of all the heartache through which they had gone, and accepting that his wife was approaching the menopause, Robert knew that they must think about the future and plan for after the baby's birth. He decided that the only way to ensure that the same situation did not arise again was for him to have a vasectomy (male sterilisation).

He told me, 'I did not come to this decision lightly. It is a form of emasculation. All of us have our pride. My wife had been willing to listen to my side of the abortion argument and alter her own thinking. Now I felt that it was up to me to take the initiative, to do my part. I requested a vasectomy and on receiving an appointment to see a consultant, my wife and I went together. I was turned down on the grounds that my wife was pregnant and could possibly change her mind after the birth, especially since she had already changed her mind over the abortion. I was asked to re-apply six months after the baby was born. I pointed out that by the time I could actually have the sterilisation my wife could well be pregnant again. The reply even now fills me with horror and disgust. I am not a violent man, but I could quite easily have hit him when he said: "You can always ask for an abortion." '

What is happening in our society when those who are called physicians have so little regard for human life and human emotions themselves? Where has any sense of vocation gone?

Fathers cannot just disassociate themselves from their own flesh and blood. After the birth, where the child is legitimate, the law holds the father more accountable than the mother for the upbringing of their son or daughter. If a baby is as much a human being before birth as after, the unborn child should be entitled to full human rights, including the right to have its father's legal protection. Something has gone wrong with British justice.

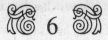

6

The Biblical View

'Vicar in "murder" outburst', proclaimed the headlines in the local newspaper. The vicar's 'outburst' was actually an extremely intelligent and well-thought-out lecture to the local LIFE group meeting on the evils of abortion. What he was saying was only what Christians have believed all down the centuries. Yet our society is so indoctrinated with the belief that we have a right to kill the unborn child, that his standpoint was condemned as 'outrageous' by the press.

A spate of correspondence followed in the newspaper, with officials and doctors from the family planning clinic protesting that every woman has a right to abortion if she requests it, and that women are best served by the law and ethics of the medical profession rather than by their own 'prejudices'. (So it seems that some doctors admit that women are still sometimes prejudiced against abortion.) The vicar was judged to be naive for suggesting that anyone could live in this modern age by biblical standards. When I asked him if he was surprised by all the furore, he seemed not to be. He admitted that the Church has so often failed to give a lead and churchmen have not spoken out as they should against this taking of life, preferring to be 'trendy'.

It is not naive to believe that today's Christians can live by the standards set in the Bible. Although civilisation has changed, human nature has not. Only in the Bible can we find the cure for the ills of the spirit and soul of a person.

The Bible does not say much specifically about abortion, although life in the womb was sacred in Old Testament times. The ancient Hebrew law laid down that:

> If men who are fighting hit a pregnant woman and she gives
> birth prematurely but there is no serious injury, the offender
> must be fined whatever the woman's husband demands and the
> court allows. But if there is serious injury, you are to take life
> for life, eye for eye, tooth for tooth, hand for hand, foot for
> foot, burn for burn, wound for wound, bruise for bruise
> (Exodus 21. 22–5).

This recognises that an unborn baby and a mature man or
woman are equally valuable. It is also significant that Luke,
who was a doctor, in his account of the meeting between
Mary and Elizabeth, uses the Greek word *brephos* for the
unborn child or embryo. This is the word that is also used
for a baby or young child. There is no distinction.

> At that time Mary got ready and hurried to a town in the hill
> country of Judea, where she entered Zechariah's home and
> greeted Elizabeth. When Elizabeth heard Mary's greeting, the
> baby leaped in her womb, and Elizabeth was filled with the
> Holy Spirit. In a loud voice she exclaimed: 'Blessed are you
> among women, and blessed is the child you will bear! But why
> am I so favoured, that the mother of my Lord should come to
> me? As soon as the sound of your greeting reached my ears,
> the baby in my womb leaped for joy. Blessed is she who has
> believed that what the Lord has said to her will be accom-
> plished!' (Luke 1. 39–45).

Elizabeth's heartbeat must have quickened in excite-
ment when Mary arrived to see her. (No telephone to say,
'Cousin, I'm on my way!') This passage tells us when the
baby leaped for joy in her womb, she was filled with the Holy
Spirit. Over six months pregnant, she would already have
been feeling her child's movements. This was not a first
fluttering or 'quickening', that suddenly thrilled her, but a
unique maternal experience, hence the ecstatic way in
which she spoke of it to Mary.

With our finite knowledge, how can we even begin to guess at what happened in the wombs of both Elizabeth and Mary when they met, both expectantly excited and yet over-awed, completely humbled at the great things the Lord was accomplishing through them and the lives of their babies? Elizabeth, well past child-bearing age, expected a child who was to be the forerunner of the Messiah, Jesus. Mary was carrying under her heart the very Son of God himself. Is it inconceivable that the first should naturally worship the second, when in close proximity? John the Baptist, the forerunner, was unique, as we are each unique, with a special place to fill, a special job to do. Mary's child was unique in a wholly new way, because he had been conceived by the power of the God, who created all that is and was and will be, through the power of his Spirit. This had to be, in order that he could enter into human life and human experience in its entirety, from conception to death. Is it any wonder that Elizabeth's child leaped with joy to acknowledge him? It is not quiet in the womb. The mother's heartbeat and the vascular rhythms and functions of her body create a noise level of up to ninety decibels, equivalent to the sound of traffic in a busy street! As Elizabeth's heartbeat quickened, as the adrenalin flowed, her baby was no doubt similarly excited.

But even in the womb Jesus was a live representative of God, a light to the world, and Elizabeth's baby leaped also at this instinctive knowledge and the need to worship him. How? How do birds know how to build a nest or travel thousands of miles across the earth in migration? How do bees know how to build a honeycomb? God has put such knowledge deep inside his creation.

Jesus was Lord, even in the womb. Elizabeth too recognised this when she burst out with a benediction on her cousin and the child within her:

'Blessed are you among women, and blessed is the child you

55

will bear! But why am I so favoured, that the mother of my Lord should come to me? . . . Blessed is she who has believed that what the Lord has said to her will be accomplished' (Luke 1. 42–43, 45).

Elizabeth had great faith that the Lord's promises to her and to Mary would be honoured. She also had great insight when, filled with his Spirit, she acknowledged that Mary's coming child was 'my Lord'. The personal prefix seems to herald a new way, or New Covenant (Testament) brought about by the coming of the child – a more personal approach to the Godhead than previously, as personal belief in Jesus would link men and women to their God.

The Christ-child is called 'Lord' even before his birth. 'My Lord' is a surprising title for an unborn embryo, but Elizabeth was very close to God, very receptive to his will and his leading, and very conscious that he is the Author and Giver of life, especially that new, long-denied life now leaping within her.

Many of us believe that because life is unique to each one, every person has a place in this world, a purpose to fulfil. We may not have been called to great things: most of us are ordinary people whose worth lies in being someone's sister or brother, son or daughter, father or mother; someone's secretary or milkman, labourer or solicitor; someone's friend, adviser, neighbour or confidante. The poet Donne says that every person's death leaves each of us the poorer. God has so arranged humanity that we all depend on each other. We depend on others physically: for our food, our manufactured goods and our health care. Mentally, we need other people's books and music, ideas and art. Spiritually we need help and encouragement, teaching and challenge from the other members of the Church, as well as power from God himself. We are that curious blend of three: body, mind and spirit. There is within each of us that strange longing for something or Someone better than ourselves, and we have that inner capacity to foster and encourage our highest ideals. Spiritually we are as individual and unique as we are mentally and physically. We each respond to God in many different ways and through diverse channels. Paul said: 'Do you not know that your body is a temple of the Holy Spirit, who is in you, whom you have received from God? You are not your own; you were bought at a price. Therefore honour God with your body' (1 Corinthians 6. 19–20.)

Today, society spends millions of pounds repairing and restoring man-made 'temples' because they have been built to the glory of God, yet is destroying countless living 'temples' containing his Holy Spirit!

Jeremiah testifies in his opening chapter:

The word of the Lord came to me, saying,
'Before I formed you in the womb I knew you,
before you were born I set you apart;
I appointed you as a prophet to the nations' (Jeremiah 1. 4–5).

The biblical message is clear, that God gives life from conception, that he has loved us and cared about us, designing our individual lives somewhere in his timeless infinite eternity; then, in an instant, at conception, his plans for us start. He gives us life: physical, mental, spiritual, just waiting to grow and develop '. . . until we all reach unity in the faith and in the knowledge of the Son of God and become mature, attaining to the whole measure of the fulness of Christ' (Ephesians 4. 13).

Thus, any violation perpetrated against the unborn is perpetrated against a human being and against God himself. Before Jeremiah was born he was designed, consecrated and given the necessary stamina, physical and spiritual, to attain what God had in mind for him. God did not see him as an inanimate blob of jelly or foetal tissue, or whatever other phraseology we now use for the unborn child. God saw him as he intended him to be: a prophet speaking out boldly on God's behalf about the issues of the day, often in fear and trembling, but always in the knowledge that God would give him the words to speak and the will to endure as he had promised. Like the pro-Life supporters today, he preached an unpopular message; yet in spite of everything, God was there when he needed him. Spiritually and physically (Jeremiah 38) he sank to the depths at times, but time and again he was lifted up to speak out about the evils of the day.

We can find other Bible passages to show that God created us 'from the beginning' for his own, and to fulfil his work on earth.

The Psalmist said:

> For you created my inmost being;
> You knit me together in my mother's womb.
> I praise you because I am fearfully and wonderfully made;
> Your works are wonderful,
>   I know that full well.
> My frame was not hidden from you
>   when I was made in the secret place,
> When I was woven together in the depths of the earth,
> Your eyes saw my unformed body.
> All the days ordained for me
>   were written in your book
> before one of them came to be (Psalm 139. 13–16).

When God promises to send Jesus to be the Messiah of Israel and the salvation of the world he proclaims through the prophet:

> Listen to me, you islands;
>   hear this, you distant nations:
> Before I was born the Lord called me . . .
> And now the Lord says —
> he who formed me in the womb to be his servant
> to bring Jacob back to him

and gather Israel to himself . . .
'It is too small a thing for you to be my servant
to restore the tribes of Jacob
and bring back those of Israel I have kept.
I will also make you a light for the Gentiles,
that you may bring my salvation to the ends of the earth'
(Isaiah 49. 1, 5, 6).

The Bible also tells us that God is a just God. What about
his judgement? Was the vicar right when he called abortion
'murder', or is it 'legalised killing'? because of the 1967
Act? As Christians, we must adhere not to the man-made
law of the land, but to the law of God: 'You shall not
murder' (Exodus 20. 13). Does God judge where man turns
a blind eye?
Isaiah asks:

'Can a mother forget the baby at her breast
and have no compassion on the child she has borne?
Though she may forget,
I will not forget you!
See, I have engraved you on the palms of my hands' (Isaiah
49. 15–16).

Some other modern versions, for instance the New Eng-
lish Bible, translate the second line as: 'or a loving mother
the child of her womb?'
So if a mother forgets, God does not forget. He has the
names of all his children engraved on the palms of his
hands.

God is able to do infinitely more wonderful things than
men. Can you believe that all the aborted babies' names are
recorded on the palms of his hands, along with yours?
The hands of God are also scarred by the nailprints of
Calvary. There is spiritual and mental healing for all who
come to God through that cross; it is not only the mothers

who must receive forgiveness. Gail, a Christian nurse, likened the medical profession's collusion and support for abortion to the back-up Hitler had from his doctors, enabling him to carry out his programme of mass slaughter. This nursing sister of a large city hospital said, 'The medical profession is aiding and abetting wholesale destruction of human life. How far would Hitler have got without the co-operation of his doctors? The unborn, the weak, the physically and mentally handicapped and those of opposing views were only able to be exterminated because of medical collusion.'

In 2 Kings 8. 12, the prophet Elisha weeps because of what he sees in the future:

'Why is my lord weeping?' asked Hazael.
'Because I know the harm you will do to the Israelites,' he answered. 'You will set fire to their fortified places, kill their young men with the sword, dash their little children to the ground, and rip open their pregnant women.'

And the prophet Amos proclaims:

This is what the Lord says:
'For three sins of Ammon,
even for four, I will not turn back my wrath.
Because he ripped open the pregnant women of Gilead
in order to extend his borders' (Amos 1. 13).

Politicians equally share in the responsibility for liberal abortion laws. In George Orwell's *Nineteen Eighty-Four* the Ministry of Truth is in charge of propaganda, while the Minister of Love organises the secret police. The dishonest fallacy promoted by mass propaganda that has replaced the sanctity of life ethic with a 'quality of life' for 'your own good' has Orwellian overtones. When we read of 'therapeutic abortion', we wonder what kind of therapy it is which kills a life.

The Bible teaches that to love means to be responsible.

When Christ was asked what was the greatest command-ment he answered: 'Love the Lord your God with all your heart and with all your soul and with all your strength and with all your mind'; and, 'Love your neighbour as yourself' (Luke 10. 27).

The exposition of that superb sentence would take another book, but to summarise briefly: when we love somebody we go all out to please that person. To love God with all sides of our nature, physical (strength), mental (mind) and spiritual (heart and soul), naturally leads to putting any other person's good before our own. If the unborn child is a person, as other biblical passages indicate, then that baby is our 'neighbour' and needs protection. On being asked 'Who is my neighbour?' Jesus told the story of the Good Samaritan. Anyone, of whatever age, creed, colour, race or persuasion, who is weaker and needs our care and help in any way is our neighbour.

From earliest civilisation pregnant women have been given priority in natural and national emergencies. Whenever the idea of 'survival of the fittest' crept in, as in Roman times, the Christian Church took a firm stand against it. And it has maintained this stand all through its history, with most of its great writers and thinkers discus-sing the subject, and all agreeing that life in the womb is sacred.

Jesus always highlighted the place of children, not only in the family, but in the kingdom of God, that kingdom of love in the hearts of people. He went so far as to say that no one could live in that 'kingdom' unless they were childlike (NB not childish).

A child is trusting. A child is honest. A child sees through adult deception. A child is not easily fobbed off with a falsehood or contented with mere theory.

With our increasing knowledge of intra-uterine life, succeeding generations will see even more of the miracles of life developing before birth. How will the Church of this century be seen in the future? As a body which maintained biblical and ethical standards? Or as a community which condoned world-wide killing by standing on the sidelines and doing nothing? How will God himself judge us? Remember those words of Edmund Burke: 'All that is necessary for the triumph of evil is that good men should do nothing.'

In Mark 9. 42 Jesus, after bringing a child into the centre of the gathering, warned that if anyone caused offence to one of these little ones, being drowned with a millstone round his neck would be preferable to God's judgement. The Greek word here is not *brephos*, but the word meaning a child/boy/servant. However, it does show Jesus' regard for children. There can be no greater offence than denying them life!

The Bible is all about loving and taking responsibility: God's love for us and his responsibility to get us through; and our love for him and for others for whom we are responsible. 'You can't have one without the other'; as with love and marriage they go together. We also take responsibility for our own activity or inactivity on behalf of weaker members of the human race, for whom we are accountable to God. He will surely judge us, individually and corporately, over the greatest toll of human life the world has ever known: approximately four hundred killings a day in Britain alone.

We have seen that the Bible upholds the view that human life is sacred, because we are made in the image of God and he loves us. Our bodies are the temples of his Holy Spirit. We have seen, too, that life begins at conception and that Christ himself was addressed before his birth as 'Lord' by a pregnant lady 'filled with the Holy Spirit'. These were not emotional words, but the speech of a devout woman full of God's love and his Spirit.

Is it so outrageous then, to say, that for a Christian, abortion is murder?

When enough of us are willing to stand up and be counted, such a statement will stop hitting the headlines as something unusual.

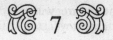

The Medical View

Those who profess Christ are not the only ones who are pro-Life supporters. There are many who would label themselves atheist or agnostic, who agree that life is sacred and should be protected, and that it begins at the moment of conception. There are, throughout the world, Christians and non-Christians working in medical practice and research who are unhappy at the way medical ethics are being undermined in all areas of medicine.

As the whole spectrum of research and experimentation has widened, many doctors and nurses have changed their position on abortion. For example, Dr Bernard Nathanson, a self-confessed 'resolute atheist', supervised the largest abortion clinic in the world, the Center for Reproductive and Sexual Health in New York City. In its first year, over 60,000 abortions were carried out, and the gynaecologist grew increasingly worried as more knowledge about fertilisation and intra-uterine development was made available. It was science alone that convinced him that human lives were being destroyed. Dr Nathanson then courageously publicly reversed his views and joined the pro-Life lobby, taking full responsibility for the part he had played in repealing the existing laws of New York State and allowing abortion on demand. In 1971 the Center was set up, like something straight out of *Nineteen Eighty-Four*, with the Orwellian paradox that the most prolific abortion clinic was called 'Center for Reproductive and Sexual *Health*'! Furthermore, clients were referred by the Clergy

Consultation Service, an organisation of some 1200 ministers and rabbis. It was a five-million-dollar-a-year business. A hundred and twenty abortions were performed daily, including Sundays.

This eminent gynaecologist now puts all his energies into trying to undo some of the damage, but he knows that he cannot bring back those 60,000 lives. After his change of conviction, he had to endure threatening letters and telephone calls and ostracism by former colleagues, neighbours and friends. With Richard Ostling, he published a book in 1979, *Aborting America*, in which the pro-abortion forces were exposed. In it, Dr Nathanson admitted that 'We fed a line of deceit, dishonesty, of fabrication of statistics and figures, we coddled, caressed and stroked the Press, in order to knock down those first abortion laws in the State.'

As this gynaecologist's story confirms, there are Christians and scientists who are now allied in their statements that life begins at conception and is as sacred in the womb as outside it.

Many people in British hospitals and laboratories today are realising the pressures and the problems. Gail, the Christian nursing sister mentioned previously, remarked that abortion needs the co-operation of the medical profession and gets it, to the detriment of our society. She was one who went through midwifery training unquestioningly. Somewhere along the way, though, disturbing thoughts surfaced and she has increasingly moved her position to one of complete opposition to abortion, and is now out of midwifery and working with chronically sick children.

Many Christian doctors are moving away from gynaecology and obstetrics. This is sad, since a Christian presence is needed there; but the bonus is that many of them are going over to paediatrics, an area where the Christian and pro-Life doctor is needed more than ever, because new-born handicapped babies are being allowed to die by non-treatment or non-feeding. More doctors with a reverence for life are needed here and this movement is providing them.

Although pro-Life doctors are under great pressure, there are many who speak out firmly against abortion. They spread the word that our society has gone too far in choosing who has a right to live and condemning others to death. One Christian doctor to whom I spoke had been out of general practice for several years, having her children. On returning to the surgery, she finds herself worried by current trends. She says she is not convinced that these days there is ever a medical reason for abortion. Very rarely is the mother's life in danger. Before the 1967 Act, that was the only reason to abort. Most abortions today are performed for 'social' reasons, usually when contraception has failed for one reason or another. The ease or otherwise with which a woman obtains abortion depends on the personal view of the gynaecologist. This doctor believes that many women are pressurised to abort their babies and deeply regret it afterwards. She told of a lady who had nightmares for months after her abortion and was in great distress for a long time. Other women, she had noticed, 'became like a stone wall', making it impossible to get through to them with advice or counselling, however sympathetic. This 'stone wall' reaction where feelings are bottled up seems most dangerous. Feelings have to be released somewhere, somehow. This doctor went on:

When the mother has been in contact with rubella (German measles) many doctors seem to over-react. There seems a panic to refer for a termination. The degree of abnormality doesn't seem to come into it these days. Because a baby with the least suspicion of possible future handicap can so easily be aborted, it bothers me that the baby is not examined after the termination to assess what might have happened. The word 'handicap' immediately conjures up horrible pictures in

66

parents' minds at a time when there is emotional stress and physical discomfort. It is only later, after the abortion, that they begin to wonder about the degree of handicap and whether they would have coped after all. Guilt feelings then set in. Some mothers have said to me, 'They made me have it done!' Yet at all times the mother is in the driving seat. No one, doctors, parents, boyfriend or husband, can make her have an abortion. We need to impress on young mothers that it is their decision and theirs alone.

'The pressure is there, though, isn't it?' I asked her.

Yes, especially for rubella contacts, also for older mothers. If a pregnant woman is around thirty-six now she seems to get an awful lot of screening. The pressure is on to take the baby's life for the slightest cause. I think people should be told much more than that their baby 'could be handicapped'. They should know more about what leads to what. There is never enough time for a gynaecologist to talk to a mother properly, but pregnant women spend time in hospital waiting rooms. Surely there could be literature for them to read to explain handicap and the possible consequences, so that if they wished to ask further questions they could. This would reassure rather than alarm, if done properly. Some handicaps would no longer seem so frightening to mothers.

While most Christians are against abortion, the word 'handicap' also seems to convey horrible mental pictures for some people in the Church. Some take the view that it is un-Christian to subject a person to maybe a life sentence of ill-health, physical handicap or mental subnormality. The doctor said:

People tend to forget that accident or illness can cause severe handicap also. The Christian should not put quality of life before the sanctity of life, although the pressures are there, the results of mass indoctrination to this theory. Taken to its ultimate conclusion, the Christian would then have to sanction euthanasia for severely handicapped victims of accident or illness. This is the slippery slope we can so easily jump on, when saying that abortion is ethical for handicaps.

I believe that even a severely handicapped baby, one who may only live for a few hours, days, or weeks, can help a parent more than abortion can. To hold such a child, to cuddle him, know that you have given him every chance, by bringing him to birth, gives a feeling of peace after the natural period of grieving has passed. That grief is more healing than the grief of abortion. To know that you have done all possible and that you have loved him, helps you to come to terms with the impending death of a child such as this. Hospital staff are only now realising the needs of newly-bereaved parents, and looking for the best way to help them in their grief. The Stillbirth and Neo-Natal Death Society (SANDS) has done much to publicise this and to educate hospital staff. Parents are now encouraged to hold and cuddle babies not expected to survive. Photographs can be taken. This is more positive than abortion. Recognised or not by the mother and her family, there is always a period of grief after abortion. It is an unnatural end to a bodily function, causing psychological reactions. Mothers watch other people's children of similar age to the baby they would have had, just as mothers do after giving up a baby for adoption.

'Acknowledging the pain of giving the baby up, what is the difference in a mother's choice of abortion or adoption?' I asked.

The pain of giving up a child for adoption is not as great as the ultimate pain of abortion, because of the hope for the future. The mother who decides that she is not capable of bring up the child, who decides on adoption, knows that her baby is going to have a far better future, with two parents, probably more adopted brothers or sisters and more material things than she can provide, as a one-parent family. With abortion, there is none of that hope. There is nothing but emptiness and often regret.

The reader may think that it is easy for this doctor to say that all life is sacred, even handicapped lives. She does, however, know the problem and pain from living with handicap, as her brother has multiple sclerosis. In an age when there is so much more help for handicapped people from medical science and technical advance, it seems strange to her that there is mounting pressure to eliminate them from our society. Whatever happened to the Hippocratic oath?

The old tribal medicine man had a dual role: to save life and to kill. This meant that although in an emergency his services were sought, his patients never really trusted him. It all changed with Hippocrates, who has been called the 'father of medical ethics'. He defined the doctor's role as that of healing and his oath has been taken by the profession ever since that time. It categorically states: 'I will give no deadly medicine to anyone if asked, nor suggest such a counsel and in like manner I will not give to a woman a pessary to produce abortion.'

In this century we have moved back to the primitive ethics of the medicine man or witch doctor, with worldwide abortion on demand, followed by increasing talk of euthanasia, prefixed by the word 'humane'. To many of us it seems that doctors are ignoring the Hippocratic Oath, turning it into a hypocritic oath.

At the Annual Conference of the British Medical Association in July 1974, the meeting recommended that all medical schools in the country should consider including in their degree ceremonies the World Medical Association Declaration of Geneva, 1948. This states:

I solemnly pledge myself to consecrate my life to the service of humanity. I will give to my teachers the respect and gratitude which is their due: I will practise my profession with conscience and dignity; the health of my patients will be my first consideration; I will respect the secrets which are confided in me, and I will maintain by all means in my power the honour and noble traditions of the medical profession; my colleagues will be my brothers; I will not permit considerations of religion, nationality, race, party politics or social standing to intervene between my duty and my patients; I will maintain the utmost respect for human life, from the time of conception, even under threat, I will not use my medical knowledge contrary to the laws of humanity. I make these promises solemnly, freely and upon my honour.

This was overwhelmingly supported because doctors were concerned about the situation under the Abortion Act and the threat of possible legalised euthanasia.

I cannot see how the promise 'I will maintain the utmost respect for human life, from the time of conception, even under threat, I will not use my medical knowledge contrary to the laws of humanity' can be twisted to allow any doctor to sanction abortion on demand. Obviously, others thought the same. In October 1983 at the thirty-fifth WMA Conference in Venice, Italy, the words 'from conception' were changed to 'from the beginning'. That slight shift in language seems to have salved some consciences, and makes it imperative for us to define the 'beginning' of life. Not only gynaecologists but obstetricians and hospital sisters have been disturbed. Many nurses have told me of horror and total shock when assisting at their first abortion. Some expected a 'blob of jelly', and the trauma of seeing a microscopic baby was severe.

While some people press and petition for legal action, and others steer legislation through Parliament, it is still the ordinary people who have to implement the law. The practical outcome of the Abortion Act was one of horror for many nurses who care about human life. For the others, indifference to the sanctity of life has been fostered and has spread, along with the notion that man plays God. For them it is a true return to a pre-Hippocratic era.

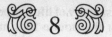 8

Is Abortion Ever Justified?

Are there any justifiable reasons for abortion? Rape?
Incest? Handicap? Where the mother's life is in danger?

It is as well here to note recent statistics. Just under 95
per cent of all abortions carried out in Britain today are for
'social' reasons. The other 5 per cent are for handicapped
babies. The question of danger to the mother's life is,
thankfully, extremely rare these days: only 0.08 per cent.
In any case, danger to the mother's life has never been an
argument for abortion on demand, since it was always
legally permissible.

Only rarely does rape result in pregnancy. The figures
are miniscule. There could be physical reasons for this:
tubal spasms occurring in the victim as a result of fear; the
rapist not being able to function sexually (a condition which
can lead to rape as the rapist tries to prove 'he is a man');
or natural infertility on either side. In the exceptional case of a pregnancy resulting from rape, many doctors,
psychiatrists and counsellors are not convinced that the
added trauma of abortion directly after the ordeal of being
raped can be good for the mother. What about her unwanted pregnancy? As has been mentioned before, nature
gives time for a woman to come to terms with the birth of
her child. This baby would be half hers genetically and all
hers by reason of the father not being interested in its
future.

Having said that, this in no way diminishes the very real
fear and heartache caused to the victims of the rapist, and

their families. But with sympathetic counselling, the victim of rape has often been able to have the baby, to keep or offer for adoption. The child is the innocent result of a violent act. Is it right that it should be denied life? That life was made by God exactly as was yours and mine. Some people feel that to abort or abandon the child would be a real case of 'the sins of the father being visited on the children'. After a discussion of this heartbreaking dilemma on American radio, a woman telephoned one of the speakers to say that she was the result of a rape. An intruder had tied up her father and raped her mother in front of him. The doctor and hospital were willing to abort the resultant baby, but the woman's husband refused to consider it. The lady said, 'I don't know how many times, as I lay secure in the loving arms of my husband, I have thanked God for my wonderful Christian father.'

Two wrongs have never yet made a right.

In 1938, in the United Kingdom, Dr Aleck Bourne performed an abortion on a fourteen-year-old girl, in severe shock after she had been raped. He gave himself up to the police afterwards, was tried and acquitted, on the grounds that he had saved the girl's sanity.

The findings of that court became the criteria for future 'hard cases' and Dr Bourne was appalled to see how this thinking was gathering momentum, leading to a climate of opinion where there could be abortion on demand, which became fully legal with the 1967 Act. This so worried him that he was one of the founder members of the Society for the Protection of the Unborn child, that same year.

But what about the 5 per cent of abortions because of handicap? There is no way of assessing the potential of a baby, no guide as to the degree of handicap, no way of forecasting a person's quality of life as we forecast tomorrow's weather. Many people alive today know that they were only just born in time: now they would have been routinely aborted. As the Christian doctor quoted in the previous chapter said, the aborted baby is not examined to establish the validity of the diagnosis. Countless women, told that there was a chance they would have a handicapped child, have subsequently produced a physically perfect baby. What constitutes handicap today? What are the criteria for gynaecologists? What are the pressures on women?

Robert and Richard, quoted in an earlier chapter, objected to the current attitude to women over thirty-six. It is not so long ago that the critical age was forty. These women, as we have seen, are fed the handicap line, yet the risk of a handicapped child is smaller than the risk attached to amniocentesis, which can produce a miscarriage. It is the way doctors can detect some evidence of about 100 of the 2,500 genetic disorders known today. This test seems to be used more as evidence to abort than anything else these days.

Our Christian doctor also talked of 'panic' over rubella contacts. In the last analysis, it is the parents who must bear the burden, either coming to terms with abortion and the psychological trauma of always wondering whether they did the right thing, or opting for the life of their child and coping with the results.

Nobody pretends that it is easy to bring up a severely handicapped child, whether the handicap be mental or physical. Handicaps resulting from rubella contact bring much extra hard work for the parents, but all those I have spoken to as I have been writing this book are unanimous in their agreement that these lives *are* worth living, that they do bring joy to their families. None of them regretted not having an abortion.

One friend of mine says: 'This is our child, part of our family, and we love her and care for her just like the others.' When a younger child was born to them, normal this time, they had double the joy from charting her progress. Each new step in development seemed so much more wonderful to them and they were grateful to God for this 'bonus' child, unplanned but so good with her older handicapped sister. They have nothing but praise for the special school their daughter attends, where once in a while she is able to spend a week's 'holiday', to give the family a chance to catch up on some rest. (Many such children are hyperactive, noisy, but full of life and laughter.)

It costs families, it costs society to cope with handicapped children, but other sections of the community are equally costly in money and care: one-parent families, children beyond the control of their parents, prison inmates, drug addicts, alcoholics all make demands on the state and its resources. Many of their problems are caused by psychological handicap or imperfections, but do we kill them? Of course not! We care for them and try to help, to bring out the best in them. A Methodist minister, chaplain of the local hospital for the mentally handicapped, said,

'I think people like these have so much to teach us. We're only just coming round to that realisation. We have always thought it was they who should learn from us.'

This reminded me of the words of Paul, that God has chosen the weak things of the world to confound the things that are mighty. Perhaps we feel that the handicapped should be eliminated because we cannot understand them. What we cannot understand, we often fear. We are confounded by them, not knowing how to treat them, how to approach them or what to say to them. With the mentally handicapped it is particularly difficult, even for those people who are used to the problem. Because they are unable to communicate, society has for so long shut them away, lumping them with the mentally ill. Now, with stories such as that of Joey Deacon, we are beginning to accept that many people we label ineducable have much more potential than we give them credit for.

Joey was the man whose story amazed those who saw it re-enacted on television or who read his book *Joey*, which took him fifteen painstaking years to write. For years after the death of his mother, who could understand some of the noises Joey made, no one could communicate with him. After the deaths of his stepmother and his father, he was consigned to a mental hospital where he worked alongside a friend called Ernie. Over the years Ernie began to understand him and was able to interpret, so that Joey could talk to other friends and staff. This association was interrupted for three years, when Joey was in hospital with tuberculosis, but it was during this time that he decided to write a book. He could not write, but his other friend Michael could, whilst a fourth member of the 'family' learned to type with one finger. These four friends spent twenty-five years together and for fifteen of them they worked on the book, often only managing a few words a day, as Joey told Ernie the story of his life and Tom and Michael recorded it.

Joey's story has opened up new hope for progress with people we label mentally handicapped just because they are unable to communicate in the way in which we do. What pain and frustrations we must have imposed on them, through our ignorance! How can we assess what they are thinking and feeling if they can't tell us? If they have used their fists or feet to try to hammer home a point, we have labelled them violently sub-normal and subjected them to an even greater degree of isolation and indifference. Helen Keller's story did a lot to change attitudes, but we still have a long way to go.

Gil, the mother of a handicapped teenager, said to me, 'How do we know that my son doesn't think that it is the rest of us who are handicapped? We do strange things like walking and running and babbling on endlessly to each other. No wonder he laughs at us!'

I invited Gil to share her story:

I am the mother of a handicapped child and a statistic of the

76

1967 Abortion Act. Richard is sixteen and lives in a specially adapted home in the north-east run by Dr Barnardo's. He is a strikingly good-looking young man with a devilish grin and an equally devilish nature to match.

He was born to me on a bitterly cold Wednesday afternoon in January 1969. Adam was to be his name, but I knew the minute I looked at him that he was no Adam. He was quickly re-named Richard.

In the two-and-a-half months that followed Richard's birth, he was a model baby, a joy to have around, waking and feeding at the right time, just like the glossy magazines said he should. Nothing, however, could have prepared me for the event that was to take place on an equally cold day in April, when my perfectly healthy baby was no more. In his place lay a motionless rag doll.

'A brain haemorrhage,' they said. 'If he survives he'll be nothing more than a cabbage.' Could this be my son they were talking about? The same son I had held in my arms a few hours previously? The same son who had protested loudly at being bathed, and then chuckled at the funny faces I pulled? Yes, this was he. Only now he would never be the same; nothing would ever be the same again.

Richard was to stay in hospital a little over two months. In those crucial first weeks I kept a constant vigil at his side. All I could do was look helplessly at his tiny, motionless body. I was eighteen at the time, and it just didn't sink in that he was spastic. All I wanted was to take my baby back home again. Unable to use his limbs, Richard did however begin to smile, to laugh again at those faces I pulled. Richard smiled then, he smiles now, only now it has turned into an infectious laugh. Richard's laugh was to become his trademark, a laugh that was to say, 'I'm glad to be alive.'

My story isn't one of heroism, of total dedication working on his helpless limbs: just of the fight for both of us to survive when the odds were against us.

Indeed it would take a book, not this short piece, to write of the years between that cold April day and the contrast of the warm summer day when Richard was to leave the love and security of his own home, to live in a place more adapted to his needs.

In those years I had given birth to two healthy baby girls. We had all come to accept, with fortitude and love, the difficulties of having a handicapped person around. We had given Richard our total energy, our every minute, love and devotion. He gave to us equal love and hours of fun. He was to show us so many, many times in those years that he was glad to be alive, and we were glad to have him.

I can never recall any bitter feelings, nor the usual cry of 'Why me?' Instead I clung like an ivy to a tree, to the knowledge that this was my destiny, and that I would meet it head on like a bulldozer meets a brick wall. Why not? Richard already was!

Although Sara was growing at a faster rate than Richard, and doing all the things he should have done, I never compared the two. After all, here were two very different children with different purposes in life.

So why then, did I decide that it was time that Richard moved on, at the tender age of six years? Well, I never did claim to be a martyr. Sara wasn't getting her rightful attention and Claire had already made her noisy entrance into the world. Along with the fun Richard brought, and the tremendous values he gave us, he also slowed down their progress and took away their share of attention. I never doubted Richard's right to live, and had always fulfilled my role as a mother happily. It was to dawn on me though, very painfully, that it was time to play full-time mother to my two little girls. To this day I can think of no other decision I have made with so much soul-searching and so much heartache. Nor can I think of one that hasn't had its repercussions. This was to be the exception. I knew I had made the right decision.

Richard developed as a child and now as a young man, and the girls had their freedom to grow too. Richard never lost his sense of fun, nor the will and the right to live. If he and others like him can live happily in this world, then shouldn't we happily let them? Handicapped people always come to terms with their disabilities and accept them. It seems that it is society that has difficulty in accepting them, due to the fear and embarrassment of not knowing how to treat them. I can well appreciate this, because even now I have the same difficulties in knowing how to approach an unknown handicapped person.

When my day of judgement comes, I for one will thank God for Richard, for the values he brought me, for the love and laughter he still brings. My world has certainly been a better place for knowing and loving him, and I am sure that if you were to ask him, he would have no complaint, because Richard has fought for his right to live.

Later, Gil also had an abortion. She continued:

The only real regret I ever had over Richard, was that my husband and I never shared the same views. We were never able to converse about him because of my husband's attitude. He believed that Richard suffered frustrations, but I maintained that he was coping with his limitations. It was this same inability to discuss our problems or see eye-to-eye about them, that led me to the doctor's surgery and eventually the surgeon's knife. Oh, I'm not blaming him entirely and excusing myself. I am just trying to point out that other people, no matter how strong we are, can manipulate us and steer us in directions we may not really choose to go. I must however add that I encountered no opposition from the medical profession either. I thought at the time, 'How can I possibly cope with yet another child?' Claire was only a few months old. Now I think, 'How could I have got myself into that position in the first place?'

It wasn't really until the two very painful years before the break-up of my marriage that the full horror of that abortion really hit home, a horror that has remained with me long after the pain of my eventual divorce.

79

However I can see no reason for dwelling on one's misery when something constructive can be done with it, which is why I have written articles on abortion and the misery it can cause. I have never made any apologies for what I have written and I don't intend to start now. Abortion isn't something you can pretty up and make look good. I believe that if you take abortion in the cold light of day, you have killed. Just take the woman (forgetting her circumstances) and the foetus. Take away that foetus and you have taken away life. For this there can be no justification.

Whilst Richard was living with us, I came across a lot of women who had been offered abortion on the grounds that they were carrying handicapped babies. Some had the abortions; some did not. Some gave birth to what society calls abnormal babies. All, however, had one thing in common: life. Despite their varying degrees of disability, they all led equally happy and fulfilling lives. None were a particular burden to society or to their parents. All brought joy.

Some, despite what was predicted, had perfectly normal babies, who also brought joy.

Much has been written of the pain of unwanted pregnancies outweighing the pain of abortion. What utter nonsense! To me, that is a convenient excuse slotted in to make us feel better. The pain of an unwanted pregnancy cannot be disregarded, but oh, what joy can be gained by creating and giving life, no matter what. No one should ever kid themselves that abortions are not painful. We can only block out the pain temporarily, with those all-too-familiar excuses: 'It's for the best!' 'It could have been a cabbage.'

As in my case, it can be years before the reality ever hits home, but, believe me, it always does. You see, I too, have stifled my conscience with those excuses and suffered the heartache they bring.

Please, just pause for a moment and think: if we could ask the foetus whether, given all the facts, it would live or choose to die, would it choose death? The joy of creating life is a beautiful one. For me, there is only One who can choose our fate for us and I see no reason to change that.

In view of that last sentence, I asked Gil if she had a strong faith. She told me that her faith in God's presence always with her was what kept her going. This, she testified, turned even the most tragic of times into times of hope, when each little bit of fun or laughter was accentuated, and changed sorrow into a worthwhile experience, through which God strengthens us.

'Ah,' you might say, 'but what about the people who had to take over the care of Richard when Gil could no longer cope at home?' It is easy for me to say that abortion is *always* wrong, but some people have to have the care of those whose lives we say are worth living.

Over the years I have known people who live with, care for or train those suffering from differing degrees of mental retardedness. In every case they have said that the struggle and achievement are more rewarding and far outweigh the problems and difficulties. There are the laughs and the love to restore the balance.

I visited Gillian and Andy, a young couple who have worked with handicapped children in hospitals and schools.

Gillian now cares for a group of children with the mental age of about a year. She told me:

You don't see them as abnormal. They are just different individuals. People say to me, 'Isn't it depressing?' but it's exactly the reverse because they're so spontaneous, living for the minute, whether it's demanding something they want or enjoying an experience that so many of us would not even see. They have an uncomplicated directness, which is *real*. It's so much more refreshing than the falsity of 'normal' behaviour, hemmed in as we are by our inhibitions and sense of propriety. It has taken us to unnatural lengths to hide our true selves, but these children have no guile. They are innocent, fresh, sweet-natured. Of course there are the problems, but you have to get to know a handicapped person and once you do that, you only see the individual, not the handicap. That word puts up a barrier to start with. These people are just different. We can't understand that, so we fear them and put up our own barriers and inhibitions. You can get so much closer to a child like this than to 'normal' children. They are so loving and have so much to give.

I make it all sound glowing, don't I? I am fully aware of the problems, but the achievement outweighs them.

I went to Gillian and Andy with two specific questions: Do you work with these children because they are there and someone has to do the job? and Are these lives worth living?

It was unnecessary for me to put those questions. From the moment that Gillian showed me into the warm and loving atmosphere of their home, her enthusiasm and joy shone from her eyes. She is literally a 'glowing person', and I can well understand the charisma which encourages her children slowly to respond to her. I had heard of her love for her group and I asked her why she chose her career.

I didn't. I trained as a teacher, but at that time jobs were fewer and I took a 'temporary' job as a very junior nursing assistant in a hospital for mentally handicapped people. I stayed four years and worked with severely disabled people, victims of rubella. Some were very disturbed: adolescents going through all the bodily changes which they were unable to understand and which we could not adequately explain to them. There were resultant tantrums and it was very hard work, but there was the fun, the happy times and the spontaneous laughter. After four years I felt I needed a break. I took on one or two jobs, for example working in a bookshop, but there was no sense of purpose or fulfilment. Admittedly I worked with people, saw lots of people, but it was not a *human* job.

Gillian emphasised the human side all the way through our conversation. There are those who consider the mentally retarded as less than human, and this *human* (not *humane*) emphasis from Gillian, stopped me from asking what she thought of the sub-human assessment. It would have been sacrilege, almost, to put the question!

Gillian teaches a group of eight autistic children who are unable to speak or communicate as we do. Mentally they are babies and progress is extremely slow. Gillian is unable to assess just how much they take in. She has to work at gaining their trust, teaching them to ask the basic things, through sign language, such as requests for the toilet, for a drink, and so on. She is never bored because no two minutes are the same. The spontaneity she speaks of leads them to all kinds of reactions to things that you or I would miss.

A shaft of sunlight suddenly shines through a window and one will go and lie on the floor where it shows. This is so lovely and so right, to enjoy being in the light, to acknowledge the sun. When we put a record on, they respond with every ounce of their energy, whereas music just washes over many normal children and they don't take in much of it. Some are psychologically impaired and disturbed and you find yourself always trying to unravel these little mysteries. It's so challenging that you are never bored. In those other jobs I did I was bored. It took that two-year break to show me that this was the job for me. I couldn't wait to get back to it.

We complicate life so much, but they don't. They have no memory of harboured slights or jealousies. They are just honest, simple, open and so very loving.

'Teaching them each day, you obviously have a deep relationship with the parents. What effects do such children have on families?' I asked.

'Mostly they pull them all together, because there is no room or time to be selfish . . .' she started.

'But they can break families up . . .' Andy contributed.

Yes, especially if other children are not getting their share of attention. It's so hard to compete with one of these 'little angels' in the family, one of the innocent little baby-children, who do not understand about being naughty. Some have such beautiful complexions and eyes and are noticeable. Ordinary children find it hard to be normal. Mothers, too, sometimes feel a kind of guilt that they did not produce a perfect baby and then go on to spoil the handicapped child, which is not good for the child or the rest of the family. It certainly makes the school's job harder. Every big problem puts strain on a family. Some split up but I think the key thing is acceptance. Once the situation is accepted by the parents, the other children, then it's a positive thing and can be worked at. That involves accepting the child in his or her own right, as an equally valuable member of the family. There are so many different spokes in this great wheel of human living. There are different people, different aims and values. The important thing is that we all slot in somewhere. We each have our place. These people are meant to have their place too. They can respond so naturally to real life, life in the raw. It's getting down to the nitty-gritty working with them.

When we have our little 'sing-songs' with David [the Chaplain] it is so unbelievably moving that it is the nearest I have ever been to a spiritual experience. They can't sing the words, but they know what is happening. They shake their shakers and bang their tambourines. David plays the organ and it's all so joyful and spontaneous. We usually end up by singing the prayer of St Francis, 'Make me a channel of your peace'. All the hospital gathers for this and those who can understand know that this is worship. I'm sure these children know too. They are so close to reality.

But what of the parents of children such as Gillian teaches? I spoke to Jean, whose sixteen-year-old son has always lived at home, attending a special school/hospital. It is eighteen miles away, but to judge from David's progress, is well worth the journey. This teenager is inarticulate, doubly incontinent, blind, epileptic, and mostly in a wheelchair, only able to walk a few steps with someone's help, never on his own.

Jean and George have three sons. The first two were ten and thirteen when David was born, a month prematurely. He seemed underweight at birth and Jean noticed one limp arm, but was told by hospital staff that there was nothing wrong with him. The doctor thought Jean a fussy mother.

When David was four and a half months old, Jean was able to get him to an eye specialist; then he was admitted into hospital. Six weeks later he had convulsions and was not expected to live. The fits went on and on and have never stopped. David has had every type of fit possible. He was hospitalised again but no one seemed able to help him. He went into status epilepsy and was eventually put into the care of a good local paediatrician who worked hard on him and gave his parents invaluable guidance. He had two years of medical treatment and exercise. His first school pronounced him ineducable, and he was subsequently taken each day on the eighteen mile journey to the special unit qualified to deal with him. The paediatrician could hold out no solid hope that David would make any progress or live long. At first Jean would look at him and wonder if he would be still with them for Christmas or Easter or the summer, but she learned to live one day at a time, and enjoy all the good parts of each day.

Ten years on, she says, he smiles and knows quite a lot of things. Although blind, he cocks his head on one side and seems to be listening when the birds are singing. His great love is travelling, so he does not mind the journey to school. He has been in trains, boats and cars and shows great delight. Jean and George took him to the Birmingham Catholic Handicapped Children's Fellowship and there met many marvellous people who understood their problems and gave them practical help and much love and care. At the regular meetings there, problems can be shared and worked out. Jean testifies that once you allow yourself to love a handicapped person a new life opens out to you. She and George have met so many people they would not have known but for David. His birth changed the whole course of their life.

Friends are real friends, not just acquaintances. They understand your difficulties and miss you if you are not there. A phone call assures you that they care. David is beautiful. He has fair hair and big blue eyes. We were very extravagant and had a gorgeous picture of him painted on canvas. We call it 'our Rembrandt'. The man who did it was so patient because David can't sit still. He has mioclonic jerks and has to take a lot of medication, but he is such a happy person. He has changed so many people's views about handicap because he is so gentle. I think perhaps that is what his job is in life, to show others that handicapped children are beautiful.

I've always been a Christian and church people always told me I was living with a saint, in David. I did so want him to be confirmed as a church member in his own right. He had always attended church with us. He sings in his own way when everyone else sings. Always during the Lord's Prayer, he claps his hands. When he has been taken to the Methodist church and Salvation Army children's gatherings with the school, he has been noticed and everyone has remarked that he is obviously a regular churchgoer and understands and participates in worship.

My church did not feel able to confirm him in his own right, but because of his association with the Fellowship, David was confirmed into the Catholic Church. When the priest touches his lips, he knows it is for Communion and opens his mouth. Everyone is so loving to him and I was able to change to that church too. I may have changed my church, but I have not changed my God. How can any of us say how much he can take in about God? I just know that worship is a part of his life and helps him as well as me.

David cannot physically see what we can see, cannot race around a football pitch, but he is excited by travel, is a communicant Christian, puts up with all his physical problems like a saint and worships God in his own way. God is not tied to our language. He understands, as David tries so hard to say 'Amen'. Who are we to assess his spiritual or mental awareness?

At school they work hard with him to try and co-ordinate his bodily movements. He goes donkey riding and loves splashing about in the therapy pool.

Last year he fell and broke his hip, but he is now back to his limited walking with help. He almost died then; his breathing stopped, he had successive fits and his bowels stopped working, but he has recovered so well. We are thankful that so much is done to help him. Every seven weeks he spends five school days as a resident, sleeping at the adjoining hospital so that he can undergo tests and monitoring of his blood, because of the drugs he has to have.

Jean and George and their first two sons have pulled together as a family and now that David has two sisters-in-law, the circle of love has widened. There were initial problems, in the early days, with the boys not liking to bring their friends home, but that soon passed, because there was enough love and acceptance to cope.

Obviously the last sixteen years have been demanding ones for David's parents:

The first sadness of having a handicapped child never quite leaves you, but our lives would have been so much poorer without David and the marvellous people we have met through having him, at the school, hospital, church and fellowship. Everyone pulls together. I can see no reason for any child to be aborted, nor for a new-born baby to be killed, especially in these days when there is so much help and advice for parents like us.

My faith is my mainstay. God gives me the strength to live one day at a time. Each day it is a privilege to have David. We didn't dream that we would have him for so long. It's a joy to thank God that he has come safely through another day, in spite of numerous fits, seizures and his other problems. He laughs such a lot. He is happy and glad to be alive. He loves everyone and gives so much to us all.

Gillian, too, had used the word 'privilege' in describing her work with such children. She also said, 'They are so innocent. We have complicated the world . . . I suppose all these choices make it so much worse: to choose the Pill or not; to have children or not; to test for handicap or not; to abort or not . . . It would be so much easier without all these choices.'

But they are there. If God has blessed us with the ability to think and reason, if he has relieved us of the burdens of mental handicap such as Richard and David carry, then we have to bear the psychological problems of choice and its repercussions.

Gillian also saw 'acceptance' as the key. When we can accept our own weaknesses, of whatever form, as well as the weaknesses, mental, physical, or spiritual, of others, we can be humble enough to learn more of God's ways. To go back to 1 Corinthians 1. 27. The Authorised Version reads: 'God has chosen the weak things of the world to confound the things which are mighty.' The New International Version translates this as: 'God chose the weak things of the world to shame the strong.'

The strongest case I ever heard or read of for the value of the life of a handicapped person in the context of 'quality of life,' was a 'True-Life Experience' in the *Christian Herald* weekly magazine (18 October 1984). It was written by a man who had decided to become a priest through the witness of a young man whom he described as 'one of God's jewels'. Roy had a brilliant mind trapped in a severely handicapped body. Born without legs or buttocks, his chest turned sideways, causing a gigantic hump in his back, he spent all his life in hospital, abandoned by his family as a freak. Tubes were always attached to him, so that he looked like a human spider. He never complained, and gave love and understanding to everyone. He had a strong faith and complete surrender to God. He died when he was nineteen. His life was a blessing, the writer claimed, which touched many through the clarity of his faith. This was not a mentally handicapped person with a simple faith, this was a man with a brilliant mind, working out his faith in spite of the limitations of a useless body. That resultant faith had absolute clarity.

Today we need clarity as we face choices which, as Gillian says, only complicate our thinking. God used Roy to lead a man to the priesthood. Every life has a purpose. Some of the weakest are needed to shame the strong, for as God also said, 'My power is made perfect in weakness' (2 Corinthians 12. 9).

9

Is This Life Worth Living?

It is surprising what 'treasures' are unearthed within the pages of *Christian Woman* magazine! I first 'met' Alison Davis there and gained a rich friendship and a year's work! Without her help with research and checking, I would not have been able to put this book together.

Alison is thirty, happily married, National Organiser of the Handicap Division of the Society for the Protection of the Unborn Child, and a founder member of Disabled Women for Life. She has a university degree, runs a home, and travels extensively, having visited Europe, the USA, the USSR, India and the Far East. At home she travels all over the country lecturing in universities and hospitals, speaking at schools and at rallies on the pro-Life cause: a hectic enough life for anyone, but Alison does it all from a wheelchair. Born with spina bifida and doubly incontinent, she has been called a 'non-person' to her face! This was by a member of the pro-abortion lobby. Today, an unborn child with Alison's degree of handicap is routinely aborted. She is very much aware that, had screening been available before she was born, she would have been just another abortion statistic. 'As it was, when I was born, the doctors were suggesting that babies like me should be left in the hospital to some nameless fate and that the parents should "go home and try again".' Yet, she insists, 'I am very happy to be alive, as are most handicapped people. She has never wanted to 'end it all', and her childhood was not 'terrible'.

We have talked of developing bodies and developing

spiritual experience. The third dimension is the mind, which develops as we learn, through school, college or university; through reading, discussing, debating, the media, and so on.

Alison, like many women of her age, was thinking and developing simultaneously with the emerging women's liberation movement. She had always had to fight for her rights, to be accepted in her own right. People have strange attitudes to the handicapped. They tend to lump them all together, failing to distinguish between physical and mental handicap, and either ignore them, talking at them and not to them, or look down on them. (I have always thought that wheelchairs should be designed to be elevated when stationary, so that the occupant can be looked straight in the eye, without having to be looked down on first. Our body position seems to have some psychological effect on our conduct!)

Alison joined the women's liberation movement and took the whole package into her system: equal rights, opportunity, pay, free contraception and abortion on demand. She believed that women could only be free if they were allowed to control their fertility as easily as men. Having now come round to the view that abortion is murder, she admits that she can well understand why some women, particularly disabled women, still support abortion. Like her, they do not know or want to know what it is and how it is performed. They are also ignorant of the very early development of the child in the womb.

One day Alison read an article about a couple who had 'allowed their baby daughter to die', encouraged by the doctor that it was 'a loving thing to do'. She was appalled, and was especially horrified at the way in which this 'loving thing' was done. The baby was sedated until it was too sleepy to cry for food and thus starved to death. The reason given was that she would always be doubly incontinent and would never have been able to walk. Alison was incensed because this was exactly her own degree of handicap. She cut out the article, but hid it away in a drawer and tried to forget it. It continued to haunt her, however, and now and again she was drawn back to it, re-reading it and getting more angry and confused.

Two years later another article finally moved her to action. She read that the killing of handicapped new-born babies in this way was 'acceptable' and that doctors were increasingly drawn to it. This time she was furious enough to write to the *Guardian* newspaper. The response was unbelievable: mountains of letters from individuals and pro-Life groups, including Women for Life, all containing relevant literature. Alison slowly ploughed through it all, reluctantly, because she did not like what she was reading: that infanticide and abortion were linked, that life began at conception, that the very earliest stages of pregnancy were unfolding a miracle of creativity. All of this pointed to one conclusion only: no one could ever achieve equality in society without first achieving an equal right to live, to be born.

Very slowly and reluctantly Alison realised that she had a vested interest. She had been incensed, not because a baby had been destroyed, but because it had been a handicapped baby, a baby like she had been. (Alison's parents had been told before her birth that she could be a cabbage!) But what about abortion for 'normal' babies? What about a woman's right? Here was discrimination in reverse. How could she fight for life for the handicapped unborn and new-born, but deny it to all the other normal babies being aborted every day?

She changed her mind about abortion and about the women's movement. 'We cannot allow our selfishness to blind us to the facts, even when they are unpalatable,' she says. She joined Women for Life and the Society for the Protection of the Unborn Child, became the National Organiser of their Handicapped Division and more recently has helped in the founding of Disabled Women for Life. Pro-Life work *is* her life now, travelling and debating, writing and discussing, counselling and filing. Draughty British Rail guards' vans are endured in sub-zero temperatures where trains have not been adapted or designed for wheelchairs. Her husband is marvellously sympathetic, supporting her all the way and prepared to take over the cooking, care of the home and household pets when she is away.

Alison believes that handicapped people and their families are the 'only true *experts on handicap*', and it is for this reason that she is tirelessly involved in putting across their point of view. In a letter published in the *British Medical Journal*, 30 June 1984, she protested:

Am I supposed to be less of a human being because my legs don't work? If not, why should the lives of those like me be considered so inferior that they are better terminated at the earliest possible moment? Parents these days are given a choice and are not forced to abort a handicapped baby, but they have to make the choice on the basis of considering the disability in a vacuum, which is unrealistic. I am not 'spina bifida' with 'Alison Davis' as a subsidiary attribute. You cannot talk about any disability in isolation from an individual who has it, yet this is what parents are being asked to do when they are given the choice of 'therapeutic' abortion . . . Who does pre-natal screening benefit? The parents get a dead baby, the doctor kills his patient, and the baby (who might well have been as glad to be alive as I am) is aborted. Who is left to benefit? The only possible beneficiary I can imagine is society in general, which is spared the 'economic burden' of caring for a handicapped person. Wasn't it Hitler who said, 'The masses will always follow that person first who offers the most impertinent promises in economic matters'? Some advance!

Alison is deeply concerned that distressed parents are

being persuaded to consent to so-called 'therapeutic abortion' without knowing the full facts. People are being duped into believing that their child's life will be miserable. Taking the therapeutic argument to its logical conclusion, all the world's diseases could be prevented by killing the patients; but surely, she argues, the response of a civilised society should be to try to alleviate all suffering rather than kill those it perceives as suffering. She makes no claim to putting forward a Christian argument – in fact, she admits to having no religious belief – but simply a sound human response: 'and interestingly enough, one of the few things guaranteed to make almost anyone miserable is to be told that they should never have been born at all.'

Alison's argument was never more forcefully put than in an address to thousands of people attending a mass pro-Life rally in London's Hyde Park:

I'm sure everyone here must be aware that handicap has become probably the most publicly acceptable reason for abortion. In fact, of course, it's so popular that it's no longer just acceptable, it is positively encouraged for pregnant women to be screened as a matter of course to discover if their babies will be handicapped and then be offered what is called a therapeutic abortion if it is.

I've thought long and hard about that word 'therapeutic', but I still fail to understand it. I've had lots of different kinds of therapy over the years, but therapeutic abortion is the only one I know where the aim is to kill the patient. Nevertheless, society seems to have decided that it *is* desirable to eliminate handicapped people at the earliest moment and I can think of few concepts so frightening than saying that certain people are better off dead and may therefore be killed *for their own good*.

I'd like you to bear this in mind, while I consider what this enthusiasm for getting rid of the handicapped means for those living with handicaps now, and what it will lead to in the future, unless people can be made to realise that most handicapped people are in fact glad to be alive and prefer, many times over, life with a handicap to no life at all.

One of the main things this enthusiasm for aborting the handicapped has led to, I'm sure you'll be very sorry to hear, is an unfortunate and increasingly common malady in paediatricians, namely a combination of poor memory and poor sight when faced with *born* handicapped babies.

These poor afflicted doctors, with the best of intentions of course, seem to forget that handicapped babies need to be fed and then fail to see that they are dying of starvation . . . or so they would have us think. Incredibly, some people are taken in by all of this and those who think the handicapped really are better off dead call it the 'agonising dilemma' of the doctor. But I say that we should beware of this kind of misplaced sympathy. Doctors *do* know what they are really doing is killing babies because they are handicapped and therefore considered unwanted, and it's vital that we should make people aware of this fact, particularly now that pressure groups are suggesting that doctors should be permitted to dispose of handicapped babies up to a month old. Once this was accepted, of course, it's not difficult to see where this could and almost certainly would, lead. After all, if we can kill a month-old handicapped baby, what about one whose handicap is discovered after two months, or a year or ten years? What about old people who are no longer considered 'useful' and who, we manage to persuade ourselves, 'had no worthwhile quality of life anyway'. How can anyone be so blind to the dangers inherent in saying that anyone has no right to life?

I believe this is an issue of fundamental human rights, which must be recognised as such by thinking people of every religious persuasion, as well as those like myself who have no religion. Discrimination on the grounds of race and sex, which limits people's liberty, has already been fought and legislated against, yet when the Disablement Bill (Prohibition of Unjustifiable Discrimination) was debated in Parliament, it failed to get a second reading and the Minister for the Disabled himself maintained that it was quite unnecessary, because there was such 'overwhelming goodwill for disabled people in this country'. If killing us off before or after birth is his idea of goodwill, then give me bad feeling any day!

It is not just our liberty that is at stake, you see, but our very lives. We must spare no pains to expose this emotional claptrap for what it is, bearing in mind the words of Martin Luther King, who said: 'Morality cannot be legislated, but behaviour can be regulated. Judicial decrees may not change the heart, but they can restrict the heartless.'

'Allowing' the handicapped to die is usually done in the name of preventing the untold misery handicap is supposed to cause, so when I first became involved in the pro-Life movement I was full of optimism that at least doctors couldn't use that as a defence when confronted by me, a happy spina bifida adult. I sadly have to tell you that I was wrong. For instance, one doctor, on hearing me say that I was happy and glad to be alive, made the incredible observation that no one can judge their own quality of life, and that other people might well consider a life like mine miserable! Another all too common reaction is to maintain that I am somehow exceptional and that everyone else with a disability *is* so miserable they would rather be dead. Of course the slightest examination of the facts would prove both these viewpoints wrong, but they are nevertheless important because they are so widely held, and because people seem to fall so easily into the terrible trap of assuming that quality of life can be forecast like the weather, or that human beings are interchangeable clones, instead of unique persons with infinite value and worth.

The doctor who tried to tell me that I was so miserable, but too brave (he probably wanted to say 'too stupid') to admit it, was making the mistake, common to many able-bodied people, of thinking that those born with a handicap must constantly and miserably yearn for the health they never had. Some do, of course, but the vast majority manage to accept and live with their limitations, and in any case, physical ability is simply not a reliable gauge of happiness. If it was, we would find ourselves facing the ridiculous notion that people who wear glasses are slightly less happy than those who don't, or that Olympic athletes are supremely happy, while people like Helen Keller supremely unhappy and unfulfilled.

In fact, I think it is an interesting fact that most handicapped people are quite content with the quality of their lives, and it's the able-bodied who are putting forward the view that handicap 'must' cause misery, because they can't imagine how they themselves would cope with it.

To single anyone out as exceptional is just ducking the issue, because if some of today's doctors had their way, no one as handicapped as I am would get the chance to live at all, let alone be exceptional. Many spina bifida babies with my degree of handicap are given only water now until they die, and although, as I have said, doctors have consistently tried to persuade both themselves and the general public that this is not *killing*, I'd like to bet that they would change their minds if we did it to them!

My own life has been full and happy, despite my disability, and the many operations it has entailed, and while I have always despised the 'ever smiling cripple' caricature as a patronising stereotype, I'm still unashamedly glad to be alive. So, too, are the vast majority of handicapped people, and in view of this I think it's time that society as a whole woke up to the fact that we have the same right to life as everyone else, and that 'therapeutic' killing, whether before or after birth, is the ultimate discrimination.

The present policy of eliminating the handicapped is defended for all sorts of reasons, but the one fact often overlooked – which I believe to be a universal truth – is that every person is unique, and therefore has an equal right to live out their life from conception to natural death, whatever their condition. Handicapped babies are being killed now because someone has decreed their 'imperfect' life is not worth living, yet no one is perfect and there will never be another one like any of us, handicapped or not.

Even though my limitations may be rather more obvious than some, that does not mean that I don't have the same capacity for life and love and happiness as anyone else. If I have that capacity, so do the handicapped babies who are being 'therapeutically' put to death now and so do those still to be born. It is just up to everyone who really cares about human rights to make sure that they are allowed to live long enough to prove it.

10

The Rights of a Child

The conceptus can be defined scientifically as a human being. As has been seen, the original Greek text of the New Testament uses the same word, *brephos*, for a born and an unborn baby. Does this then entitle the unborn child to full human and legal rights?

The Preamble to the United Nations Declaration of the Rights of the Child states:

> Whereas the peoples of the United Nations have, in the Charter, reaffirmed their faith in fundamental human rights, and in the dignity and worth of the human person, and have determined to promote social progress and better standards of life in larger freedom,
>
> Whereas the United Nations has, in the Universal Declaration of Human Rights, proclaimed that everyone is entitled to all the rights and freedoms set forth therein, without distinction of any kind, such as race, colour, sex, language, religion, political or other opinion, national or social origin, property, birth or any other status,
>
> Whereas the child, by reason of his physical and mental immaturity, needs special safeguards and care, including appropriate legal protection, *before* as well as after birth . . .

That seems to be plain enough.

There then follow ten principles of which I quote the relevant parts:

Principle 1   states that 'all children, without any exception whatsoever, shall be entitled . . .' It goes on to repeat the above distinctions, and again, there is no comma after 'birth'. Does 'birth or any other status' include the unborn human?

Principle 2 'The child shall enjoy special protection and shall be given opportunities and facilities, by law and by other means, to enable her or him to develop physically, mentally, morally, spiritually and social- ly . . . In the enactment of laws for this purpose the best interests of the child shall be the paramount consider- ation.'

Principle 4 'To this end special care and protection shall be provided both to the child and to the mother, including adequate pre-natal and post-natal care. The child shall have the right to adequate nutrition, housing, recreation and *medical services*.'

Principle 5 'The child who is physically, mentally or socially handicapped shall be given the special treat- ment, education and care required by her or his particu- lar condition.' Surely that does not mean having her or his life taken away?

Principle 6 The child . . . needs love and understand- ing . . . Society and the public authorities shall have the duty to extend particular care to children without a family and those without adequate means of support.' This seems to mean caring, not killing.

Principle 7 'The best interests of the child shall be the guiding principle of those responsible for education and guidance . . . that responsibility lies in the first place with the parents.' There does not seem to be any exemp- tion clause, here or anywhere else, stating that a parent can 'choose' whether or not to be responsible for a child.

Principle 8 'The child shall in all circumstances be among the *first* to receive protection and relief.

Principle 9 'The child shall be protected against all forms of neglect, cruelty and exploitation. She or he shall not be the subject of traffic in any form.' Compare this with the buying and selling of human embryos for research; with 'allowing a handicapped newborn child to die'; and with the treatment of the victims of hysterotomy.

Principle 10 'The child shall be protected from practices which may foster racial, religious and *any other form of discrimination*.' Compare this with the discrimination between a 'wanted' and an 'unwanted' baby, between a 'normal' and a 'handicapped child.'

There is now increasing concern over a proposal for a new Convention to protect the rights of the child. A representative of the United Nations Department of the Foreign and Commonwealth Office has stated that it has been decided that 'International agreement could best be achieved more quickly by limiting its scope to children from birth to eighteen years.' It seems that the 1959 Convention, which deals specifically with the need to protect the child before birth, may be set aside solely on grounds of expediency. Since the United Nations working group which is drafting the new Convention meets only once a year, this seems a weak reason. In any case, it could be several years before the draft is complete. This should in no way lull pro-Life supporters into apathy. While the UN Declaration of Human Rights was not legally binding and did not create legal rights, the new document is a legal Convention. If the UK becomes a party to it, our domestic law would have to allow us to comply with the international legal obligations arising from it. It is imperative that objections should be sent to the Foreign Office and to Members of Parliament. The first draft has already been produced. Now is the time to act.

What is current thinking about the rights of the unborn, and how much pressure is there to deny any rights at all?

Like many others, I was incensed and heartbroken over the 'Dr Arthur' case, well covered in the media (see p. 91). For many Christians this was a first insight into many disturbing aspects of medical practice in NHS hospitals. At that time, the President of the National Secular Society was reported as saying at a meeting: 'The belief that a newborn baby, or even an unborn foetus, has full human rights, is a superstitious belief based on religious ideas. That a secular court should uphold religious ideas at the expense of common humanitarianism and extend the legal concept of human rights beyond its philosophical justification is deplorable.'

The concept of 'common humanitarianism' is all right as far as it goes, but it only goes skin deep. At best it reduces the human race to a herd of pedigree animals. The word 'human' surely means an 'animal with a soul'. If the sole aim of abortion is to eliminate illness and disease, however desirable that may be, some of our greatest poets, philosophers, artists, statesmen and 'ordinary' courageous handicapped people ought not to be allowed to live. Byron, Toulouse-Lautrec, Beethoven, Alexander Pope and Samuel Johnson are among many great artists who were severely handicapped. True greatness often comes from the moral strength needed to overcome physical deficiencies.

Pressure groups like the NSS mean business. Pro-Life people need to show strength too, every single one of us. The NSS President assumes correctly that human rights arise from religious ideas. Christ himself acknowledged the dignity of all men and women. He lifted eastern women from 'beasts of burden' to full human status. His first resurrection appearance was to a woman, Mary Magdalene, a former prostitute. When we study his meeting with the Samaritan woman at Jacob's well (John 4) we can guess that had she been alive today she would have belonged to the women's lib. movement: five husbands and a lover! She may well have been emotionally incapable of sustaining a relationship. To Christ, this woman was as handicapped, as damaged, as any person born with severe spina bifida, but a few minutes in his presence and she was a whole person. He always healed the whole person, whether that person was physically, emotionally or mentally handicapped.

Where the rights of a child are concerned, we have already seen (p. 62) that Jesus warned of the gravity of an offence against 'one of the least of these'. We have to be sure that rights are needed, not wanted. We have to guard those hard-won rights that can so easily be squeezed out by expediency.

The Christian faith is an enigmatic paradox: 'Whoever wants to save his life will lose it, but whoever loses his life for me and for the gospel will save it' (Mark 8. 35). Many have given up their own selfish rights in order to take up the sacrificial way of Christ, and have found a rich fulfilment. He taught the right to love and be loved, by God and by each other. Only that is true freedom, true liberation. Christ himself knew it on the cross. He was free to choose, yet bound to accept, the way of suffering, of love.

All of us are in some way bound: by love, by suffering, by duty. When we start assessing our rights, bitterness can corrode. Each of us has a right to share Christ's suffering. How else can we share in the victory of the resurrection? Every baby, handicapped or otherwise, has a right to be a child of God. No secular court on earth should be able to take that away.

We have a situation today where human and legal rights are granted discriminately: for wanted babies; for physically perfect babies; yet the Declaration of Human Rights states: 'without discrimination'.

Pro-Life people are termed emotional when they talk of Nazi Germany in relation to abortion. Women have a choice, it is said. But the truth is that women have to choose when they are at an extremely emotional stage of pregnancy, and most who choose abortion do so for emotional reasons. The ancient Spartans exposed babies to the elements, taking them back into the home again if they were tough enough to survive. Compare this with the 'Stobhill Baby' case in Glasgow (see p. 15) and there does not seem to have been much progress in babies' rights.

Martin Luther said that Paul's letter to Philemon was put into the Christian canon because it is a 'whole social charter'. In sorting out the question of rights for the slave Onesimus, it proclaims the rights of all persons. As Onesimus' owner, Philemon could legally treat him as he liked. Yet because he was a Christian, Philemon must treat Onesimus as a brother. Philemon might have bought Onesimus with cash, but Christ had spent his life-blood for him. This gave him a priceless value.

Thomas Carlyle said: 'A loving heart is the beginning of all knowledge.' When we love, we know our rights. We have a right to put other people's rights first and respect them as our own. And babies, even unborn babies, are people. Jesus went so far as to say that we should love others as we love ourselves. That simple statement, with its limitless responsibilities, is the Divine Declaration of Human Rights. The standard is set by Christ: 'Love one another as I have loved you.'

The legal rights of the unborn are very unclear in this country with regard to abortion. It is legally possible to claim damages for injury in the womb. Once a child has been born, a parent or close relative can act on his behalf. But no one can claim for premature death before birth, or for the loss of his or her child by abortion. Legal proceedings can be brought against a doctor for performing an abortion contrary to the terms of the 1967 Act, but most breaches of the Act go unnoticed.

The legal position with regard to injustice to the unborn child rests on two words: 'in being'.

Legally, a doctor performing an abortion is not held to be committing murder because murder is defined as 'the unlawful killing of a reasonable creature *in being*'. The premise that a baby is not 'in being' until it has an existence independent of the mother comes from the writings of Lord Justice Coke, who, living as he did from 1551–1633, was quite a long way removed from modern scientific and medical knowledge of intra-uterine life! It seems ludicrous that modern law should depend on a legal definition of 'in being' so far behind the times.

Some members of the Association of Lawyers for the Defence of the Unborn (ALDU), would like to see a statutory legal definition, which would be binding on the courts, to the effect that an unborn child *is* a life 'in being' and a legal person for the purpose of the law relating to murder and manslaughter. They claim that this simple change would:

1 be in accord with scientific and medical knowledge;

2 be simple and unambiguous;

3 not affect doctors carrying out an authentic termination of pregnancy, in the original meaning of the term, to save the child or benefit the mother's health by bringing on the baby;

4 mean that defendants in any proceedings would have the same defences for murder or manslaughter, e.g. diminished responsibility, no other reasonable means of self-preservation, etc.

5 be in line with the existing civil law relating to inheritance, affiliation proceedings, etc.

This all seems so simple a change to effect, but British

law is a cumbersome piece of machinery not easily moved.

ALDU, founded by eight lawyers in May 1978, has since spread nationwide with sister organisations in other countries. Membership is open to judges, members of the Bar, solicitors, academic and non-practising lawyers, trainee solicitors, law students and legal executives. Its members accept the undisputed findings of modern embryology that human life begins at conception. They therefore hold that natural justice requires that the child, however young, should enjoy before birth the same protection of the criminal law as is enjoyed by any other human being.

The Association regularly publishes its own Newsletter, *News and Comment*, which is sent free to members, but which can be purchased by members of the public. It also arranges conferences for members on various aspects of the legal situation of the unborn child and is pleased to provide speakers for meetings of other organisations on request.

The aims of the Association are:

To uphold the honour of the legal profession by opposing forthrightly the erosion of human rights and natural justice which abortion necessarily represents.

By lucid presentation of the facts, to help all members of the profession to appreciate why no lawyer can in good conscience support abortion.

To oppose any further erosion in the protection which the criminal law still affords to the unborn child.

To strive to create a climate of opinion in the profession which will support full statutory protection against abortion for all human life from conception onwards.

I asked a member of the Association what ALDU, whose role is chiefly educative, could do to help any father in the same position as Richard and Robert (chapter 5).

He replied, 'We could put him in touch with a solicitor. Depending on the exact facts, the solicitor might well be able to advise bringing proceedings in the name of the father as the next friend of the unborn child for an injunction to forbid the anticipated injury. Such proceedings are most likely to be successful, in our view, if the child is old enough to be capable of being born alive.'

In Orwell's *Nineteen Eighty-Four*, Newspeak was the new language whereby old words were given new meanings. In the same way, 'termination of pregnancy', as we have seen, whilst formerly a medical term for bringing on a baby to birth when necessary, now means abortion.

Currently, those to whom it should matter seem to have difficulty in defining 'capable of being born alive'.

Section 5(1) of the Abortion Act 1967 states that: 'Nothing in the Act shall affect the provisions of the Infant Life (Preservation) Act 1929 (protecting the viable foetus).'

This seems to equate a 'viable foetus' with one 'capable of being born alive'; yet today, medically, 'viable' seems to mean 'able to sustain life after birth'. A new-born severely handicapped baby is termed non-viable, although it was capable of being born alive.

Apart from this definition in the Abortion Act, there is no other definition, so far as I can discover, in any statute nor in any reported decision of the courts. It seems to be an American term adopted by the medical profession, with no British legal definition, yet it has been used in the Abortion Act, the Warnock Report and elsewhere, as a guide to when a baby is eligible to be treated as 'human'. This is not compatible with modern scientific knowledge, and is a clear example of Newspeak.

The unborn baby is treated with exceptional injustice. Those who perform 'late' abortions are flouting the law. According to the terms of the 1929 Act these abortions are illegal – yet those who perform them are not prosecuted.

Each year there are approximately four thousand

pregnant schoolgirls between eleven and fifteen years old. About half of these pregnancies end in abortion. It is illegal for a man to have intercourse with a child under 16, yet these cases are not reported. In most instances the name of the father is known. The medical profession, the DHSS and the police are not following up these thousands of breaches of the law. If this were done, schoolgirl pregnancy statistics would fall dramatically. Word soon gets around the teen-age grapevine!

If the laws relating to the Abortion and Infant Life Acts were applied as vigorously as most other laws in this country there would be a marked decrease in abortion and family trauma.

If euphemisms such as 'a mother's right to choose' were clearly shown to be Newspeak, the general public would not be deceived to the extent seen today. The 1967 Act did *not* give a mother a right to abortion on demand. Two doctors have to be satisfied that the terms of the Act are being implemented. A doctor's assessment that a child *might* be handicapped is *not* a legal reason to abort. There has to be evidence of future serious handicap. Neither did the Act allow any mother to be pressurised into an abortion.

The victims of abortion are not able to defend themselves. Only those of us who were fortunate to be allowed birth and life are able to speak up for them. Nancy Hopkins in her poem 'The Innocents – Unborn', quoted at the beginning of this book, says, 'Lend us your tongues'. As early as 1933, Dietrich Bonhoeffer, agonising over abortion, frequently quoted from Proverbs 31. 8, 'Open thy mouth for the dumb'; or as the New International Version translates it, 'Speak up for those who cannot speak for themselves.'

All who care should register objections about the proposed new Convention of the Rights of a Child, asking that the unborn baby should be protected.

All who care should speak up about the blatant injustice of abortion.

109

11

The Alternatives

In a society such as ours, pro-Life supporters will not get very far in educating people that abortion is wrong, without offering positive alternatives.

When any woman is suddenly confronted with an unwanted pregnancy, panic usually pushes sense out. If rational thinking can be resumed before abortion is considered or sanctioned, it will be seen that *there are living alternatives*.

Obviously, if it is decided to save the life of the baby, the mother must go through with the pregnancy and birth. After the birth, several courses are open. There is adoption, or accepting help and support to bring up the child, either in the family, or, in the case of an unmarried mother, as a one-parent unit or in the household of the mother's family. What is involved in each of these situations and how much help is available?

There are several organisations which will provide information, advice, and sometimes practical help.

LIFE Care and Housing Trust is a registered charity offering a nationwide pregnancy counselling and care service. LIFE is a voluntary, non-denominational and non-party political association of people who are opposed to all direct abortion.

SPUC, the Society for the Protection of the Unborn Child, also campaigns politically and educationally to gain pro-Life support, but does not have facilities for residential care.

Women for Life is a pro-Life wing of the women's movement with its new off-shoot, Disabled Women for Life. They provide literature and advice from verifiable sources (usually medical papers), so the information is impartial, objective and correct.

Care Trust, under its director, Anne Townsend, is launching a national initiative to reduce abortion by offering help and advice to mothers who wish to have their babies.

All of these groups take positive action to press for repeal of the 1967 Act, monitor current medical practice and help women through the first panic of unplanned pregnancies.

Joan is a housemother with LIFE. Like most ventures, her involvement with pregnant women with problems arose out of her own experience. In Joan's case, she shared her home with the unmarried daughter of someone she knew. For four years she took pregnant unmarried girls into her own home, giving them help and support before, during and after the babies' births. The 1967 Abortion Act had spelled the end for many mother-and-baby homes. The experts had predicted that there would be no more unwanted pregnancies. Charitable groups and churches running such hostels had many other calls on their finances, property, resources and personnel. With the first drop in the rate of illegitimate births many of them wound down their provision of residential care for mothers and babies. But the need was still there. Some women have been turned out by boyfriends with whom they have been living, others by parents. Joan started with one person, and went on – and social workers and doctors became aware of her concern. When there were more girls than she could cope with in her own home – she is married with a family of her own – she dreamed of premises in which to carry on the work. When a local social worker asked if there was any way in which he could help, Joan told him of her hopes and he took her to see an ex-police house. The local LIFE group were able to lease this house from the County Council.

'Everybody rushed in to help,' Joan told me. 'A local carpet firm carpeted the place throughout. Others gave furniture and fittings, household utensils and cash donations. When somebody takes the initiative it's surprising how many people rush in to get involved.'

The house has now been in operation for five years. The LIFE group had only about a dozen members, yet fundraising help was available. At one time when they ran out of cash, local social workers said, 'You can't close. We can't manage without you.' LIFE headquarters thought the same and came to the rescue with a loan from central funds, as the house catered for such a large area. This reason alone shows the crying need for more nationwide help and support.

Joan told me that 90 per cent of the women she helps are pregnant through contraceptive failure (antibiotics or a bout of sickness and diarrhoea, for example, can cancel out the effects of the pill).

The LIFE group puts advertisements in the local newspapers, doctor's surgeries and family planning clinic offering free, anonymous pregnancy testing. Word also gets around that the group can be trusted. Social workers, the local maternity hospital, midwives and the housing department also refer girls to the LIFE house.

There are two categories of mothers needing help: the unmarried and those who are married but feel unable to cope with another pregnancy. As LIFE points out, an unwanted pregnancy does not necessarily mean an unwanted baby.

Through the free pregnancy testing scheme, LIFE counsellors are in at the very beginning, when the initial panic sets in. Joan always advises girls to do nothing for two weeks, until there has been time to think and plan. Some do opt for an immediate abortion, but they are still assured that they are welcome to go back and talk afterwards. Some do. One did after seven months, on the verge of suicide. She blamed herself, her parents who had 'made her do it', her doctor, her boyfriend who had 'got her into trouble' in the first place. Joan talked to her and also put her in touch with the Samaritans. Almost all women feel guilty about an abortion and many go on longing for another child, even up to menopausal age. They will not mention it outright. They call it 'my little operation', or 'slight internal trouble', when they need to explain their hospital visit.

Married women who feel unable to cope are given financial and practical help. The local group is a clearing house for prams, cots and most baby equipment. A group of women spend a large amount of time knitting, to keep up the stocks of layettes, as well as piles of good quality second-hand babywear. Joan has a rule that she will not pass on any clothes she would not have put on one of her own children.

Some pregnant women stay in their own lodgings, working as long as possible. Some have to be persuaded not to skip hospital appointments. Some need help with diet and pre-natal care. 'Care starts from the confirmation of pregnancy and goes on *ad infinitum*,' said Janet, another hard-working LIFE member, whose husband is also the secretary. The LIFE house takes in those with nowhere to go. If the house is full, there may be other houses with vacancies. Returns are made monthly to headquarters, so they are aware of vacancies.

Some pregnant girls are under sixteen. If the parents, products of the 'swinging sixties', pressurise them into abortion, there is nothing that LIFE can do. To take under-age girls into the house without parental approval is, under law, tantamount to kidnapping. Most parents, though, are grateful for the help the group can give. Once the pressure is off, many parents are extremely supportive.

Some keep their pregnant daughters at home up to the birth of their grandchild, after which there is no room. Every parent knows how much space a tiny baby needs, with pram, cot, bath, carry cot, and so on, not to mention drawer space for clothes and nappies. Some young mothers would have previously been sharing a bedroom with a sister. This means that some girls enter the LIFE house after the birth. A baby cannot be left at a maternity hospital without being technically abandoned, yet a mother is not allowed to leave hospital with the baby and no home to take it to.

As soon as a woman enters the LIFE house, she goes on to the local council housing list and is usually re-housed when the child is about six months old.

The house takes four women at a time. They share housework and can buy and eat separately or communally. Each has her own pantry and a bedroom with a yale key. They share the two refrigerators, the lounge, dining room and bathroom. The more experienced mothers are able to help the others, both before and after the birth of the baby.

When in hospital, if there are no relatives to visit, the girls are visited at least once a day by a LIFE member.

Joan is not resident in the house, but goes in each morning when a new baby arrives, to help with bathtime and any problems for which the mothers need advice. The residents are encouraged to attend parentcraft classes. The first six months in the house with other mothers and experienced help on hand can be invaluable to a young and inexperienced new mother. Sometimes help is needed with cleaning and budgeting and Joan teaches the mother how to prepare inexpensive but nourishing meals. This is an asset when she eventually sets up home alone.

Every month or six weeks there is a meeting to sort out such details as the cleaning rota and to listen to any grievances, and discuss any problems. Some girls will leave everything to the more willing and some just cannot cope

114

with a new baby and their share of the housework. Joan will help out until a routine is established, or help a girl turn her bedroom around. It is her experience that young mothers in the house who have been abandoned by boyfriends or family need personal love and attention, as well as practical help. There are occasions when a girl's social worker has to be summoned, but mostly Joan copes. The same problems constantly arise and although each is new to the mother, to Joan they are usually anticipated and capable of being resolved. In extremely rare circumstances, a girl has been found to be an unfit mother, for example, when she is taking drugs or going back to an alcoholic or drug-taking boyfriend, where the baby would be at risk. In these cases the child has been temporarily fostered.

The women contribute their share of the running costs of the house. It works out cheaper for the DHSS to keep them at the house than in bed and breakfast accommodation, the only other alternative. They get the added moral support of the LIFE group whose telephone numbers are listed in the house. An office is also manned each evening, for girls in need to ring in. This gives the residents a chance to talk to an experienced counsellor when the babies are settled for the night.

LIFE counsellors have to be alert and sympathetic. The first telephone call from a woman is the most vital and her confidence can be built up or broken by the way it is handled. Some young girls telephone several times, but lose courage each time the phone is answered and put down the receiver. It alerts the counsellors and they stay around, usually until contact has been established.

Joan's group applied for a council house for two girls to share, feeling that it would shorten the housing list and gently ease them from the comfort of life with other young mothers, into the loneliness of their own home. Neighbours do not always welcome a single young girl with a baby. Housing rules about sub-letting, however, proved

this scheme to be unfeasible, but Joan feels it could have
been a halfway house for her girls, while they gained more
ability and confidence. However, constant support and
visits from the group members help to combat that initial
loneliness. There is also an extremely good family centre
run by the local Anglican church, with counsellors and
mother and toddler facilities. It often takes over where the
LIFE house withdraws.

Most resident women respect the house and the system.
There have been exceptions, girls with 'all the answers', but
this is sometimes a cover-up for insecurity and an initial
distrust of the group. Motherhood matures most girls.
After the birth, some girls go back to discos and their
former haunts only to find that they have outgrown their
old interests and friends. Where do they fit in? There are
emotional scars to heal; they are wary of making new
relationships with boys. Joan has to be a good listener and
gentle persuader. She provides the love and motherly
concern they need.

Although calm and capable, Joan is visibly disturbed
when talking about abortion. She maintains that most
women do *not* think of their child as a blob of jelly,
whatever the fashionable doctrine. 'They do know that
they are expecting a baby, that it is a baby they are
contemplating killing, and when they do give in, under
pressure to abort, the guilt comes out, even if not for years.
In the end the pain has to be faced and worked through.'

Thirty-one girls have stayed in the house in its first four
years. Many more have been helped by the group outside
the house. Yet in that period over 1,500 abortions have
been carried out at the local hospital, which serves a rural
area where the abortion rate is well below the national
average. A nearby university city is served by a separate
LIFE group and house. There the figures are much higher.

This clearly shows the need for much more help and
support by all pro-Life people, to aid existing schemes or

take the initiative where there is no residential work going on. If full-time caring is not possible, individuals may be able to help in small ways, such as knitting or hospital visitation. 'Friends' are needed for such things as accompanying a nervous young girl to her first ante-natal appointment, or visiting newly-housed girls. Teaching a girl to cope initially increases her confidence, and this will help to make her a better mother.

Most girls are much more cautious the second time around and more ready to listen to family planning advice.

Joan concedes that adoption is painful, but holds that it is not as traumatic as abortion. She was almost in tears as she recalled some of the heart-searching that goes on before a mother comes to a decision about adoption: 'It is a heart-breaking decision and I don't want to minimise the pain. A girl will say, "Why should I have a baby for somebody else?" but as I tell her, she already has the baby. The question is whether to keep it or destroy it, or accept that maybe somebody else could at least give the child a home and love. A girl has to be generous to opt for adoption rather than abortion, when she knows there is no likelihood that she can bring up the baby herself. If she so decides, she comes out of hospital after two days, rather than stay in with the new mothers and babies. We provide a new layette for the baby, which is left at the hospital. Some girls do not realise that they themselves have to name and register the babies. This is often upsetting. There is definitely a period of grieving, but it is a more readily accepted grief than that of abortion because the mother knows that the baby is alive and well and going to a welcoming home.'

Joan spends a lot of time with girls after adoption and says it is the hardest part of her work. She has no part in the actual adoption. That is all handled by the hospital secretary.

Maybe you, the reader, are unmarried and find yourself

pregnant, abandoned by boyfriend or family. There are three options:

Abortion, with its psychological, and possibly physical, aftermath.
Adoption, with its pain, but hope for the future.
Bringing up the baby yourself, with the help and support of people who care. You will not be unique. One in eight families in Britain today are one-parent families. A great deal can be done to help them. This does not make it an ideal arrangement, but it is a fresh start and gives you something to work on.

Choose a *living* alternative because, for your baby, it is a matter of life or death.

For you, it is a chance to turn a painful experience into a positive hope.

Or you may be an older mother whose own family has 'flown the nest'. What next? Perhaps you are too out of touch to re-learn your former skills. You feel finished, menopausal, bored. You may not know that CARE Trust is launching a nationwide initiative to match up those in need with those with the experience to meet those needs. Anne Townsend, its Director and a former editor of *Family* magazine, gave her reasons for taking up her new position:

For the last four years, from my seat in the Editor's chair of a Christian family magazine, I've seen the increasing break-up of family life in Britain and the pressing needs of many individuals for Christian help.

As I've become aware of the enormity of the need I feel the time is right for me to stop just writing about people's problems and get out there and help others to do something.

That's why I'm leaving the magazine to establish a nationwide caring network to link people facing personal crises with local Christians who are willing and able to help . . . People with problems want someone to turn to who won't be shocked yet is able to give sensible advice and guidance, practical and biblical. Christ's love and compassion can only be expressed through the Church's and individual Christian's self-giving and sacrificial caring.

Anne is mounting a search for homes willing to take in pregnant mothers who might otherwise be pressurised into having an abortion because they have nowhere to go and no one to care. This scheme will help the mother to keep her baby.

If you think you can help, Anne Townsend is waiting to hear from you or your church. She goes on: 'Please come alongside us and help us in a vital work which we believe God is calling the churches in Britain to take on. We need you to be involved. We need your support. We can't do this without you.'

Anne told me that CARE Trust wants to launch the scheme with full caring back-up for all the family, with follow-up help, with support for the 'host' families. Meanwhile, Care Trust is working closely with CARE Campaigns in its active programme of seeking to lobby Parliament to change laws which are unbiblical.

Much is being done; more could be done with the support of the whole Church. That has to start with me and with you.

🍥 12 🍥

Action Needed Now

All of us who believe in the sanctity of life need to do whatever we can, now, in whatever way the opportunity presents itself: politically, individually, corporately; spiritually, practically or academically. The pro-Life lobby will be stronger with your wholehearted support.

If you have a say in local or national government, use your vote and your voice to promote life, not death. Invite trained speakers into your schools, your industry, your social centres.

If you hold office in your church, make sure that your members are aware of the facts. Publicise literature and invite speakers to your youth clubs, young wives groups, women's meetings and discussion groups.

If you are housebound or inactive, maybe you have more time to pray. Pinpoint your prayers:

1   Find out how many abortions are done daily at your local hospital and pray for that one, eight, ten or however many women are going through that trauma for that day. (Joan, mentioned in the last chapter, has been called to her local hospital several times because women have had doubts at the last moment, and sometimes she has been able to save the baby, assuring the mother of continued support. This could have been in answer to somebody's prayer.)

2   Pray for your local GPs and gynaecologists, that they may make wise decisions when faced with dilemmas.

3 Pray for your local pro-Life workers.

If we continue to be apathetic, what are the alternatives?
Various national groups are campaigning to legalise euthanasia and infanticide of the new-born handicapped. We
may have already aborted another Alison, whose life-work
could have been to campaign for *your* right to live when you
are eighty, or even forty or twenty if you are severely
handicapped by accident or illness. Once we begin to
choose who will live and who will die, we open the door
wide to abuse. Today you could be mugged or murdered
for your money or your property. Maybe in your lifetime it
will be legal for your family to kill you when you are old and
a nuisance and they think it is time they enjoyed your
worldly goods. After all, you had the 'right' to kill their
would-have-been brothers or sisters in the womb.

Take away the challenges that caring for our weaker
members demand of us and we are a poorer society.

Take away the wrestling in prayer that sacrificial love for
others demands, and your spiritual life will be the poorer.
Multiply this in the lives of other Christians and we will see
a weakened corporate Christian witness.

If we fail to stem the rising tide of indifference to the
miracle and creativity of life, we engender a much poorer
standard of living, both morally and ethically.

When proponents of abortion and infanticide talk of
'quality of life', they are merely speaking in material and
physical terms; but we have three sides to our nature.
Human beings have always been at their greatest when
there have been challenges that tap the resources of body,
mind *and spirit*.

As Christians, we tend to spend our time and energy in
strengthening our own spiritual lives and the lives of those
with whom we come into contact. Sometimes we can get on
the treadmill of the church calendar and routine, blinkered

from the spiritual poverty of people who rarely come into contact with Christian thought and prayer. If this applies to you, as it does to all of us to a greater or lesser degree, let us jump off and open our eyes to people in our street, our town, our clinics and surgeries.

Our communities change: cinemas are closing and video shops opening. Will there be more redundant churches or new ones springing up? Will more nominal Christians be persuaded to take on secular views, or will they become temples of the Holy Spirit? Or are we facing the prospect of those other temples, full of wooden dolls to expiate the guilt of millions of abortions? We could see more LIFE houses and counsellors, more families involved in schemes such as CARE Trust's initiative.

We cannot put *Nineteen Eighty-Four* back on the shelf to gather dust. We have to be aware of the Big Brother threats, of the Ministry of Love advocating killing as 'the loving thing to do'. We can only start to achieve universal acceptance of the sanctity of life when we set our standards high and show the need for a return to right living and right loving. There is only one place where you can start: *where you are*!

As we have looked at alternatives to abortion, we have only considered the problem in terms of caring for the victims: mothers, fathers, babies, families threatened by or suffering from abortion. We should be doing far more to prevent such tragedies arising in the first place.

The real task of the Church is to get back to preaching *right loving* as well as right living. It is as the result of an act of sexual intercourse that I exist and am able to write this, and you to read it. In the beginning, God created the world and everything in it. At our beginning, God began a work of creativity in each of us; creativity of body, of mind and of spirit (or soul).

In that superb sentence where Jesus asked us to love God

and our neighbour as ourself, we are asked to love with *all* of ourselves: body, mind and spirit.

The Church has found it difficult to give clear positive teaching on sex. This has been the great taboo subject. Those words of Paul's that our bodies are the temples of the Holy spirit, the exhortation to subdue the flesh and, the way in which the secular world has treated the subject, have all helped the church to 'sweep it under the carpet'. Wives have been told to submit unquestioningly to their husbands. For some this led to physical as well as emotional pain, secretly endured for years, while other Christians have enjoyed a rich and fulfilling relationship.

The British, particularly, have a strange capacity to laugh about that which they feel unable to discuss openly. Sex has become associated with ribald jokes, seaside postcards and shows, leading on to pornographic magazines, 'blue' films and now video nasties. While the Church has mounted campaigns against some of these, there has been no sustained effort to explore and teach the wonder of that great God-given capacity to love another person with the whole of oneself: body, mind and spirit.

We can cure some of the attitudes to abortion with better teaching, practical care and political reform, but we can only prevent it when the sanctity of sex, as well as the sanctity of marriage, is upheld.

Love has been debased in the name of sexual freedom. The act of sexual intercourse has become, in many cases, simply a means of self-gratification. In plays, films and books and for many ordinary people intercourse has casually replaced the goodnight kiss at the end of a 'date'. It has become an accepted part of courtship, not something sacred to be saved for marriage. The medical profession has condoned it, the Pill allowed it, while the Abortion Act offers the final solution for any 'mistakes'.

For too many, the purely physical act of intercourse, without the tenderness of a loving relationship, has been disappointing, leading to psychological problems which spill over to harm future liaisons and marriage. Thankfully, the Church is wakening to the problem. Books are being written, dialogue is taking place, but we have lost ground in the place where we needed to be: outside the Church.

The value of touch, of bodily contact, has suddenly emerged again as an important part of family living and loving. Breast feeding of babies is now given fresh prominence after being out of fashion for some time, because psychiatrists have realised that the love and comfort of the mother's body 'feeds' the child emotionally at the same time as it is being satisfied physically. Child experts are now saying that our children are suffering from a lack of cuddling. The flood-tide which swept over us, with its surfeit of advertising, fiction, drama and song all propounding sex, has led to paranoia about the ordinary affectionate exchanges between people. We seem to feel we must not touch anyone else, except in a mutually agreed sexual relationship – or when celebrating a goal on a football pitch! Yet in all our problems, a basic need is for someone to hold our hand; we want a shoulder to cry on. Bodily contact is therapy for many of the ills of the world. A hurt child wants his parents to pick him up and cuddle him. Our first reaction when seeing friends or relatives in trouble is to want to put our arms around them.

In the more intimate context of marriage, the importance of sexual activity does not lie only in procreation. Making love is always creative and at times it is also procreative. The Church should have been more clear in its teaching about that dual role.

Physical love-making creates forgiveness, reconciliation, healing, wonder, gratitude, warmth, passion and joy. There may also be re-creation. Take out the hyphen and you have 'recreation'. Loving intimacy can be relaxing, easing away the tensions and strains of the day, often after

124

those very tensions and strains have been discussed, talked or prayed through.

A couple can say 'sorry' through love-making, with no need of words, just a turning back to each other; the first tentative move a reaching out for love and forgiveness, the answering response an acknowledgement of reconciliation. It can say things that inarticulate people find hard to say; like 'I love you', or 'Thank you'.

People frequently hurt each other; families can hurt, society or friends can wound, but the sharing of this special act can heal the pain of other relationships, the emotional stabs from daily contacts. It can strengthen the feeling of unity and trust.

At the least, if love is present during intercourse, the other's feelings, the other's pleasure, have been put before one's own. If something has caused someone not to reach the heights, love and tenderness have given pleasure. At best, it can cause a deep cry from the heart: 'Lord, if human love can be so full of wonder, so awesome, how can we guess the depths of your divine love for us?'

Sometimes, when the other partner is not able to participate joyfully, the love it represents demands abstinence or self-control. The strength of a marriage lies in knowing each other well enough to understand when to make love and when not to.

In our clumsy human way, we have often undervalued and devalued God's gift of sexual love, seeing only the need for mechanical sex and mechanical birth control. When reduced to a momentary act of selfish pleasure, with no responsibility or tenderness attached, with no bonding together in a deepening relationship, we take sex from its natural context and abuse it, as we have abused so many of our God-given privileges.

To share a developing, creative relationship with another person, to use that relationship as the foundation on which to build a family, to create a cell of love which will

125

divide, then join with another from another family, to multiply; surely that is the pattern that God uses for human growth and creativity, the pattern of our family structure. In it we see also a pattern for the creation and spreading of love, of values, of a little bit of each of us, let loose in the world, to multiply, in a spiritual sense, after joining with the love of someone else.

We are one family on earth. God is our Father. He has designed the structures of family life and love, as well as the cell structure of our bodies. When we take part of the structure and cast aside the rest, we diminish our potential as human beings. So it is with so-called sexual freedom. In it we see the paradox of love. It is in being bound to each other that we can grow to feel secure, to be free to be ourselves, to pass on our security to our children. When we insist on being free to make and break casual relationships, we find ourselves bound by regrets and our own failures, our feelings of loneliness. Children are often the innocent results and victims. Their insecurity results in their being unable in their turn to form stable relationships.

We fight for selfish sexual freedom and we are bound.

We work unselfishly at cementing the bonds of love and we are free.

When there is a reverence for the body, mind and spirit of the other partner, a whole new dimension of creativity is released. The Church asks couples, in their marriage vows, to pledge their love for each other, their material sharing and their reverence for each other's body.

When society puts the God-given gift of sexual loving back where it belongs, at the heart of a loving, growing married life, we shall find that the abortion rate will start to drop. We are not called to expediency, to a compromise with the spirit of the age. When we preach marital loyalty, the sanctity of family life, of marriage, and reverence for the act of intercourse, we may once more begin to gain credibility outside the Church.

Our God is generous. He gives us not only food for our bodies, but flowers and butterflies to delight us. He creates millions of eggs which are never fertilised, billions of seeds which are never sown, but those he chooses to fertilise, he blesses with the infinite gift of life. Surely those, he wills to be.

On a slender thread,
packed into embryonic cells
Your will indelibly tells
The colour of our hair,
our shape of nose,
capacity to care,
our size of feet,
our talents and our flair.
No two blueprints quite the same
and on Your hand engraved each name.
But what of those
sharply curetted, decapitated,
precipitated
(in black plastic)
to cradles lined with fire?
No sackcloth . . .
just ashes of our desire,
and stain
of blood upon our palms,
and pain
of stifled guilt, along with qualms
of conscience,
as we thwart Divine Design,
abort Your creativity.

They too, were meant to be,
to live, to laugh, to see
the nailprints in Your hands
beside each name.

Dear God, abort our blind indifference,
Arouse our shame.

Addresses

Association of Lawyers for the Defence of the Unborn, 40 Bedford Street, London WC2E 9EN

CARE Campaigns and CARE Trust (Christian Action Research and Education), 21a Down Street, London W1Y 7DN

Disabled Women for Life (*see* Women for Life)

LIFE Care and Housing Trust, 118–120 Warwick Street, Leamington Spa, Warwicks, CV32 4QY

Society for the Protection of the Unborn Child, 7 Tufton Street, London SW1P 3QN

Stillbirth and Neo-Natal Death Society, Argyll House, 29–31 Euston Road, London NW1 2SD

Women for Life, 18 Ash Grove, Penge, London SE20 7RD

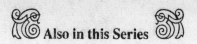
Creativity
Using your talents
EILEEN MITSON AND OTHERS

'In the beginning God created ...'
and we, his children, made in his image,
also have the desire to create.
Creativity is God's gift to us.

If therefore our lives are open to him,
he will show us areas in every aspect of life
in which we can create new growth –
our homes, families and environment,
in our relationships and in our own
personalities and talents.
He has already provided us with the raw materials –
we can use them to build or destroy –
we can choose to be on the side of life, or of death.

Nine women who have chosen life
have contributed to this thought provoking book,
which will inspire every Christian woman
to explore new ideas and to develop
her own unique creative potential.

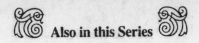

A Woman's Privilege

JEAN BRAND

The modern Christian woman
is often confused about her place in the world.
Secular pressures have blurred the
divisions between male and female roles.
Is this in line with God's plan for women?
Or does he require a woman to submerge
her whole personality
in submission to her husband?
And what about single women?

Jean Brand affirms that the Bible
represents a far more glorious pattern
and shows in a practical way, how every woman
can use her individuality and experience
to become the person God intends her to be.

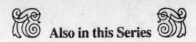

Also in this Series

Family Planning
The ethics and practicalities of
birth control methods

GAIL LAWTHER

This Christian book on contraception
looks at the options available
and is intended for Christians
who are married or planning to marry
and who wish to regulate their fertility
in a way compatible with their faith.

Gail Lawther has researched the subject carefully
and discusses in a Christian light
the methods available, their practicalities, the risks
and the advantages and disadvantages of each.
Special attention is paid to the
ethical questions involved and to the
new problems raised for Christians
by some of the most recent research.
Couples who are concerned to make the right choices
with each other and before God will find her approach
particularly helpful and informative.

Other titles in preparation